Identity Is The New Money

PERSPECTIVES

Series editor: Diane Coyle

Identity Is The New Money

David Birch

LONDON PUBLISHING PARTNERSHIP

Published by London Publishing Partnership
www.londonpublishingpartnership.co.uk

Published in association with
Enlightenment Economics
www.enlightenmenteconomics.com

ISBN: 978-1-907994-12-8 (pbk)

A catalogue record for this book is
available from the British Library

This book has been composed in Candara

Copy-edited and typeset by
T&T Productions Ltd, London
www.tandtproductions.com

Cover art by Kate Prentice

This book is dedicated to the late Professor Glyn Davies, whose outstanding book *A History of Money from Ancient Times to the Present Day* and speech at the first ever Digital Money Forum in London in 1997 together formed the bedrock for my understanding of the relationship between money, monetary policy and technological change

Good name in man and woman, dear my lord,
Is the immediate jewel of their souls.
Who steals my purse steals trash; 'tis something, nothing;
'Twas mine, 'tis his, and has been slave to thousands;
But he that filches from me my good name
Robs me of that which not enriches him,
And makes me poor indeed.

William Shakespeare, *Othello*, Act 3, Scene 3, 155–161

Contents

Foreword

There was a moment early on in the financial crisis of 2008 when, according to the then Chancellor of the Exchequer, Alistair Darling, Britain's banks came 'within hours of shutting their cash machines down'. This was a vision designed to strike fear into the hearts of families around the country: what happens when the ATMs are switched off? Millions, surely, would starve! There would be riots! Society as we know it would come to an end!

The reality would almost certainly have been rather less apocalyptic. We know as much because it has happened before. In the 1960s and 70s, Ireland's banks were shut for, in all, a year. Yes, it was messy and occasionally traumatic, but life went on. People came up with a whole range of alternatives, as they have done throughout history whenever financial or monetary chaos has stripped them of their currency or their financial system.

To point this out is not to downplay the difficulty of such moments, but to underline an important truth, which is fundamental to this book: money is a means, not an end. Yes, the notes and coins may be there in our hands; we occasionally exchange them with other people (though less and less these days); we often pay for items using our bank or credit cards. But the purpose of money in each case is to make a transaction; it's simply the token which, over centuries, humans have used as a shorthand for proving that one person is willing to transfer a certain amount of wealth, time or earnings to another.

So when money, or the financial system that perpetuates its transfer, breaks down, the world does not end – we just come up with other tokens. Rightly, however, such moments give us pause for thought about whether the current system of economic transfer is really fit for purpose. The ATMs may not have stopped in 2008, the banks were bailed out and by many yardsticks remain as powerful and influential as before the crisis.

But, as Dave Birch shows in this thought-provoking book, advances in technology in recent years nonetheless promise to revolutionize the nature of money. After all, thanks to the Internet, we are living in a world of near-frictionless communication. It is possible for anyone to correspond, and hence transact, with almost anyone else. This has enormous consequences for the medium of that transaction – not to mention the question of how one proves one's identity to those billions of potential people.

If you're anything like me, by the time you've finished reading the book you'll be wondering not just why we're still exchanging copper, zinc and nickel coins with each other, but whether the days when a country can hold a monopoly over currency are coming to an end. Such questions are not, in and of themselves, new. And there is no mass cash-machine shutdown to force us into confronting them. However, there is a compelling case that technology may now have reached the stage when they are finally answerable.

Ed Conway
Economics Editor, Sky News

Preface

While the immediate genesis of this book lay in a talk I gave to the Royal Society for the Encouragement of Arts, Manufactures and Commerce (RSA) in London in 2011, the ideas it crystallizes go back much further. In 1997, along with my colleagues at Consult Hyperion, my work in the secure electronic transactions field had caused me to reflect on payments and identity management. I had come to the conclusion that there were some major changes underway and that we needed to explore the implications. The arrival of the world wide web and the mobile phone meant that the highly secure and efficient transactions systems that we had been working on for the Bank of England, the Stock Exchange, high street banks and even a proposed space mission would soon be available to the mass market. As my colleague Neil McEvoy pointed out at the time, the secure computers, costing tens of thousands of pounds, and secure data networks, costing millions of pounds, used to execute money market trades in the City of London could be replaced by free Internet Protocol (IP) connections and the €1 tamper-resistant microprocessors now seen on every credit and debit card, swapped between mobile phones and inside every 'tap and go' mass transit ticket.

I began to wonder what this significant technological advance in monetary transactions would mean. With the strong and unswerving support of my colleagues, I set about creating the Digital Money Forum and, subsequently, the Digital Identity Forum, in order to bring together a wide range of experts to explore the technological, business and social changes each year in London. It became clear that the two topics were converging and, in time, all of the events, blogs and podcasts were gradually merged into the Tomorrow's Transactions thought-leadership blog, podcast, annual forum and 'unconference' series held in the United Kingdom and North America. The discussions, observations and reflections that stem from seventeen years of these forums, in the context of Consult Hyperion's work for clients on secure electronic transactions around the world, form the core of this book and its central claim: the future of money is linked to the future of identity.

As time has gone by, I have become ever more convinced that we need to revise our understanding of what identity is and reformulate technical, business and, above all, social strategies for dealing with identity in the 'new economy'. This book is an attempt to explain why. It also suggests one or two significant implications for policy makers and others.

My argument is, in short, that the new economy and new society that we are building on top of it demand a new way of thinking about identity, and a new way of thinking about money – and that the two converge.

Acknowledgements

It goes without saying that this book would not have been possible without Diane Coyle's support and encouragement (for which I cannot thank her enough), the intelligence, experience (and patience) of my colleagues at Consult Hyperion and the support of my wife, Hara (and her tolerance of midnight word processing).

Chapter 1

Introduction

> The chief principle of a well-regulated police state is this: That each person shall be at all times and places ... recognised as this or that particular person.
>
> Johann Gottlieb Fichte (1796)

What does 'identity is the new money' mean? My argument is that the nature of identity is changing. The concept of identity in today's post-industrial society is profoundly different to the concepts of identity that we are accustomed to, both the bureaucratic notion of identity that emerged from nineteenth- and twentieth-century industrial society and urban anonymity, and the pre-industrial notion of identity that built on extended family and clan. We might call it 'new identity' to emphasize its technological nature.

This book argues that not only is identity changing profoundly, but that money is also changing equally profoundly, because of technological change, and that the two trends are converging so all that we will need for transacting will be our identities. The technological change I'm talking about here centres of the evolution of social networks and mobile phones. They will enable the building of an identity infrastructure that can enhance *both* privacy *and* security – there is no trade-off.

The long-term consequences of these changes is impossible to predict, partly because how it takes shape will depend on how companies (probably not banks) take advantage of business opportunities to deliver transaction services. But I will predict that cash will soon be wholly redundant – and a good thing too – and there will be a proliferation of new digital currencies.

Rethinking identity

The old concept of identity is broken in the world of the new technologies. Identity is neither singular nor fixed, no matter how administratively convenient it might be to think of it that way. There are really three kinds of identity associated with people: the individual's own personal or psychological identity, their social identity and their legal identity. Neither individual nor social identities are fixed: they evolve and change over a person's lifetime; and they should not really be conflated with the legal identity. Legal identities *are* fixed and are about the identifiability of the individual.[1] Online, we have multiple social identities that may be linked directly or indirectly to our legal identity. There are different kinds of mechanisms for validating various types of transaction, and for ensuring security and privacy.

A new understanding of identity is essential and ultimately inevitable, but what that understanding is depends on the complex co-evolution of technology and paradigms. It is very difficult to predict how these will co-evolve for even a few years ahead. Technologists (like myself) tend to overestimate the speed of adoption of new technologies but underestimate the long-term impact on society. In other words, it will take longer than people like me expect for new forms of identity to reshape mass markets, but when they do the impact on society will be far greater than just making it easier to log on to the *Daily Telegraph* website. Once you begin to look more than a few years ahead, in fact, the social changes wrought by new technology become hard to imagine.

This has always been the case. For example, on 3 April 1988, the *Los Angeles Times Magazine* published a description of life now. It contained all sorts of bizarre views of life in Los Angeles today, including such unimaginable fantasies as supersonic jet travel and people smoking cigarettes. But it's a fun read, and in the true spirit of palaeo-futurism, I encourage you not to laugh at *what* the writers got wrong but to reflect on *why* they got it wrong. For example, what's wrong with this picture from the magazine story?

> Bill is trying to locate his wife to tell her about the dinner guests. Unable to reach her either at home or the office...

It has been at least a decade since my wife has called me either at home or at the office or, indeed, anywhere else. If she wants to talk to me, she calls *me*, she doesn't call a place where I might be. The mobile phone didn't just change the payphone business, it changed the communications paradigm, the common mental model that we share as the basis for thinking about communications.

Uneven

The Canadian novelist William Gibson, author of the seminal work of fiction for the new economy, the wonderful *Neuromancer*, and the man who coined the term 'cyberspace', famously observed that the 'future is already here, it's just unevenly distributed.'

He means that the technologies that will shape society in our lifetimes already exist, it's just that we might not have noticed them yet. One of the key elements missing from that

1988 vision of 2013 was the mobile phone, despite the fact that it had already existed for a decade. In fact I'm sure that some of the people writing that magazine piece had a mobile phone, but hadn't realized where mobile phones were going.

I think that the future of identity over the next twenty-five years, in common with the future of a great many other everyday tools, rests on that device formerly known as the mobile phone and what Sam Lessin of Facebook calls the 'superpower' of being able to communicate with anyone anywhere in the world at any time. Understanding this is key to shaping and forecasting the identity paradigm that is explored in Chapter 2.

When I heard the futurologist Richard Watson talking about the problem of forecasting across a generation at the Digital Money Forum,[2] he said that one of the central problems is that the kind of digital bubbles people are living in lead to a kind of Balkanization of the future. We have to look out of the corner of our eye to see how technology is being used in ways that might disrupt existing business models, and that is difficult. So this leads me to think, in the spirit of William Gibson, that just as the magazine writers didn't see that the decade-old technology of mobile phones would change the communications paradigm, that there must be a decade-old technology that is going to be pervasive in fifteen years' time, leading not just to disruption in old businesses and the creation of new ones but to a fundamental shift in mental models.

So what is it?

Social identity the new paradigm

I think the answer is social identity. I specifically do not say social media. Yes, social media are an incredible new technology. Yes, we can use them for all sorts of exciting new purposes. But it's what they are doing to identity that will be disruptive in business, commerce and government. Facebook, LinkedIn, Twitter, Tumblr and all of the others are already demonstrating just how our identity paradigm is changing. Identity is returning to a concept built on networks, rather than index cards in a filing cabinet. In common with a great many other people, a couple of billion, I use these networks almost daily. In a relatively short time, these tools have transformed society and will continue to transform it, as discussed in Chapter 3, in ways that are hard to imagine right now.

We already use these social networking identities, albeit in fairly primitive ways, to log in and browse around on the web. We could find ourselves using them for 'serious' business pretty soon. Why shouldn't I be able to log in to the Benefits Agency using my Facebook identity? This might be very convenient for me and it might be also be very convenient for the Benefits Agency, but right now the Benefits Agency couldn't really be sure it was me, because they've got no way of identifying the 'legal me' online, and neither have Facebook.

That is changing as identification and authentication technologies continue to develop. Suppose these social identities were made a little more secure. We can begin to imagine how more sophisticated and secure forms of identity might begin to change this equation. Perhaps I use my bank account to log in to Facebook, so now Facebook can be sure I really am 'Dave Birch'. Then I can use my Facebook account to log in and sign on for unemployment benefit. This would take us into a different kind of online world, a different online experience where privacy becomes an active, rather than passive, part of life.

New money

The second area of profound technology-driven change I want to discuss is money. In order to further explore 'identity is the new money', we will have to explore what 'money' means. One of the problems in discussing money is that this simple English word means several different things to economists and technologists – in the classic definition it is a unit of account, a store of value and a medium of exchange. I want to focus here on money as a generalized means of exchange between buyer and seller to enable transactions, and on money as the subset of the means of exchange that does not involve credit, or in other words, cash. Identity changes the requirements for, and use of, both kinds of money, both the pounds or euros that denominate all transactions and the transactions that still use the physical notes and coins themselves.

That *LA Times* vision of 2013 had one of the protagonists go to an ATM and draw out $20 bills. When I travelled to Austin, Texas, for the South-by-Southwest interactive festival in 2013, I didn't take any US currency with me nor did I get any bills out of an ATM while I was there. I paid for everything using cards and my mobile phone. In other words, I paid using my identity.

Time for change

This, and similar experiences, show that signs of change are already starting to be detectable. Contactless cards and mobile phones, Bitcoin and Isis, Amazon gift certificates and World of Warcraft Gold – we have the technology, as they say, and in Chapter 4 I look at the ways that it is changing money and explore the reasons why things are changing now.

The technology enables change, of course, but it isn't by itself the trigger for the shift that is coming, which will involve not only the widespread use of completely new mechanisms for exchange beyond debit cards and PayPal, but also new stores of value. We've seen a great deal of innovation to date but it hasn't yet reached the core, the institutions and, yes, the paradigms of money.

Innovations in payment technology must not be confused with the basic construction of a monetary system.[3] Ours is actually a relatively recent invention. It is barely forty, and having something of a mid-life crisis. When Richard Nixon ended the convertibility of the US dollar into gold in 1971, we entered a new world of fiat currency. From that day on, dollars have been backed by the full faith and credit of the United States and nothing more. All the world's currencies are now 'pure manifestations of sovereignty conjured by governments'.[4] That's why the talk of 'virtual currency' is misplaced: all currency is virtual.

More than a decade ago, Michael Klein, then Chief Economist of the Royal Dutch/Shell group of companies, said that monetary regimes have changed around once per generation.[5] They aren't going to stop now. It is time for another regime change.

We've been here several times before. Around four hundred years ago, things were going horribly wrong with money in England. If you had asked people about the future of money at that time, they would have imagined better quality coins. What in fact happened was revolution and a new paradigm. A generation later Britain had a central bank, paper money – although the smallest banknote, five pounds, was worth a month's pay for a professional[6] – as well as a gold standard, current accounts and overdrafts.

We are at a similar point now, with a mismatch between the mentality and the institutions of paper money in the industrial age and a new, post-industrial economy with a different technological basis for money. In a generation or so, there will be a completely new set of monetary arrangements in place. Just as the machine-made, uniform, mechanized coinage introduced by Isaac Newton in 1696 better matched the commerce of the industrial revolution, so we can expect some form of digital money will better match the commerce of the information age.[7]

Reputation and retail

So what will link changing identities with changing money as these trends converge? In a word, trust. In a world based on trust, it will be reputation rather than regulation that will animate trust in economic exchange.[8] The 'social graph', the network of our social identities, will be the nexus of commerce, administration and interaction.

In our distant past we were just as defined by our social graph as we are now.[9] There were no identity cards or credit reference agencies or transactional histories of any kind. In the absence of such credentials, you were your reputation. Of course, managing and maintaining reputations among a small social group of an extended family or a clan was not a scalable solution as civilization progressed and moved on to growing trade as the source of prosperity. In the interconnected future, however, there is every reason to suspect that the social graph will resume its pre-eminent position since, as I will explore, it is the most trustworthy, reliable aspect of a persona. This is where the link with money begins to take shape. As the anthropologist Jack Weatherford wrote[10]:

> The electronic money world looks much more like the neolithic world economy before the invention of money than it

looks like the market as we have known it in the past few hundred years.

Far-fetched? I do not think so. In 1696, there was no cash in England with the result that 'no trade is managed but by trust'.[6] With trust, you don't need cash. A wonderful example of this can be found in the three long strikes that shut down the retail banks in Ireland for months at a time between 1966 and 1976 (see the case study on page 67). The economy did not collapse in the absence of cash (which soon ran out), as personal cheques and IOUs provided the circulating means of exchange. There were, at the time, some 12,000 retail shops and (perhaps more importantly) some 11,000 public houses that provided transaction services. Antoin Murphy's seminal work on this reports:[11]

> It appears that the managers of these retail outlets and public houses had a high degree of information about their customers – one does not after all serve drink to someone for years without discovering something of his liquid resources.

Identities and credentials are easy to create and destroy. Reputations are much harder to subvert since they depend not on what anyone thinks, but on what everyone thinks. Reputations are a sound basis for interaction. People make judgements based on other people's reputations, and behave better out of concern for their own.[12] There would have been precious little chance of pretending to be someone else at the local pub in Ireland in the 1970s and as a consequence the social graph was able to provide the necessary infrastructure: the landlord knew whose IOUs were good and whose were not.

What does a modern society based on these reputations look like? I can make an informed projection in one particular area. When it comes to commerce, reputation replaces money.

Identity implications

At the dawn of the Internet age, the Nobel prize–winning economist Paul Krugman wrote that:[10]

> There will be a distinction between electronic cash and electronic money because of the need for small transactions where neither the buyer nor seller want [sic] the buyer's creditworthiness to be an issue.

This apparently common-sense distinction will vanish, which takes us to Chapter 5 of the book. If we suppose that some form of identity infrastructure comes into existence and reputation becomes the basis for transactions, then what might the implications be? It might be fun to focus on the *Tomorrow's World* gee whiz of Google glasses, but for this book I have chosen to focus on the very specific issue of electronic money for a few reasons.

Firstly, because almost all money is already electronic. In the UK, the notes and coins in circulation are a mere 4.5% of the broad money supply. New technology makes it possible to get rid of money's mundane rump.

Secondly, because losing that rump has economic implications (the existence of cash means a zero floor on interest rates and that restricts options for managing the economy), business implications (in reducing costs and reshaping retailing) and social implications (because the costs of cash fall disproportionately on the poor while the benefits mainly accrue to criminals of various sorts).

Finally, because it's fun. Everyone uses cash without really thinking about it, so picking on cash as a way of exploring the impact of new ways of thinking about identity is practical, understandable and (I so desperately hope) entertaining for the non-specialist.

With an effective identity infrastructure in place, there will be no need for a single medium of exchange, no need for fiat currency. If you know all of the counterparties to a transaction, and can establish their 'credit', then there is no need for cash. Identity substitutes for cash: when I go into Waitrose and pay with my John Lewis MasterCard, it's an identity transaction. The terminal in Waitrose establishes that I have access to a line of credit that means that Waitrose will be paid. No actual money moves between my card and the Waitrose till. On the other hand, when I buy an apple from a market stall and pay for it with a pound coin, the stallholder doesn't need to waste any time or money trying to establish who I am, because he doesn't need to trust me. He just needs to trust the pound coin, which he self-assays. It's not that there are no counterfeit pound coins, because there are, but that there are too few of them to disrupt commerce (and, to be honest, if you give the smallholder a counterfeit coin and he later detects the fraud, he will probably just palm it off onto someone else).

When managing reputation is efficient and implicit, the pound coin becomes uneconomic and so does everything that goes with it: the cash register, the ATM, the security guards. If you don't need cash registers and ATMs, then the costs and complexity associated with handling currencies collapse. If it becomes my mobile phone talking to the chap at the market stall's mobile phone, then there's no reason to restrict our commerce to sterling, or euros, or, for that matter, any fiat currency. We can use Bitcoins or Microsoft Money. We can use kilowatt hours or Brixton Pounds. We can use gold-backed e-Dinars or trade-backed barter currencies. We can use Dave's Dollars.

If you don't like their money, you can start your own. If the identity and authentication infrastructure is in place, it will be easy. Focusing on money, then, I think I can say that the impact of the new identity will be profound: so profound, in fact, that identity will be the new money.

Implications

So I argue here that identity becomes the key to transactions and a crucial individual resource that needs to be looked after by responsible organizations. We all need to start planning for the transition to identity-based transactions.

There is the social impact to be considered. We need to find a way for the infrastructure to deliver privacy and security to individuals and organizations. There should be no further discussion of the 'balancing' of privacy and security as if there is an unavoidable trade-off between them. We need both.

The business impact will be, inevitably, creative destruction at the heart of capitalism. New businesses, and new business models, will spring up to use the new technology and the new social graph.

Finally, the technological impact will shape the trajectory of new products and services. If there is some form of utility identity infrastructure that, as I hope, delivers both privacy and security to people, devices and organizations, then it should be standardized and accessible for open, transparent and non-discriminatory use.

This book ends by considering these impacts, and making three practical and positive suggestions for policymakers.

Chapter 2

Identity is broken

I am not made like any of those I have seen. I venture to believe that I am not made like any of those who are in existence. If I am not better, at least I am different.

Jean Jacques Rousseau (1712–78)

A letter in the *Daily Telegraph*'s 'Money' section (2 October 2009) sprang out at me because it exemplified the problem of identity in modern life. The letter came from someone who had tried to open a bank account with HSBC, but who didn't have a current passport or driving licence. She wrote: 'When I explained this at a branch, it was suggested that I ask the police station for proof of identity.' She dutifully went to the local constabulary, who told her that they had never heard of such a thing unless she had a criminal record. Thinking it seemed odd that you can only have a bank account if you have a criminal record, she returned to the branch to be shown a list of documents that the bank would consider acceptable for the purposes of account opening, and this time they suggested a letter from Her Majesty's Revenue & Customs (HMRC). She reports 'I duly went to the local tax office, where the assistant said she wished banks would stop sending people there... they would not waste public money providing such letters for banks.'

The letter goes on to list the documents that she had presented and had had rejected by the bank: an out-of-date passport, a birth certificate, a current payslip from an employer (the local council, for which she had worked for more than two decades), a work ID card (complete with microchip), utility bills, statements from another bank, house deeds and a voting card. Any one of these would have got you a job with the bank, but not, it seems, an account.

In a way, oddly, banks don't really care about your identity. They care about the credit history of whatever persistent persona you present to them. They are complying with stringent 'know your customer' (KYC) regulations. These have nothing to do with any real identity security. At the moment, if you come and open an account with, say, a North Korean passport, the bank cannot possibly know whether it is a genuine passport or not, but it doesn't matter, since the obligation on them is simply to keep a copy of it. If they do this, and the passport subsequently turns out to be false, it's not their problem.

On a practical, prosaic, day-to-day basis, identity is broken and we need a new model.

Police dog

Identity has been broken since the earliest days of the online world. Remember that old cartoon, 'On the Internet, no one knows you're a dog,' from the *New Yorker* in 1993? When I first started going to Internet conferences, this was in every presentation, including mine, but I was using it make a different point, which was that although in cyberspace, no one knows you're a dog, no one knows you're with the Federal Bureau of Investigation (FBI) either. Come to that, no one knows whether you're a real person or a police-controlled software agent, cruising the Net looking to ensnare miscreants in dirty deals! I said this many years before reading that this is exactly what law enforcement agencies were doing, going undercover with false online profiles to communicate with suspects and gather private information, according to an internal Justice Department document.[13] I'm not being critical: I want the police to use the Internet to catch the bad guys.

The point is to flag up that the legitimate interests of law enforcement must be taken into account when we begin to think about how identity should work. This task is actually quite difficult, because the way that identity works in the virtual world is not an analogue of the mundane world.

Multiple personalities

When it comes to the virtual world, multiple personalities are both real and actually desirable. Using different 'personae' across different types of transactions will become natural to us. Just as you use a different email address for work and personal messages, you will use a different identity in work and personal situations. This is a good thing; having only one identity that you have to use in all situations is not.

Travellers to Iran are forced by police at Tehran airport to log in to their Facebook accounts. Their passports are confiscated if they have posted criticism of the regime, which makes me wonder why everyone doesn't take the precaution of creating a dummy Facebook account in their real name. (I'm going to make one and post a paean to Iran's spiritual leaders just in case I am ever detained by Revolutionary Guards and forced to log in.) But will this be enough? Remember what happened to the British film-maker David Bond when he made his noted documentary Erasing David about trying to disappear? The private detectives that he had hired to try and find him simply went through Facebook. They pretended to be him and set up a new page, using the alias Phileas Fogg. Then they sent messages to his friends, suggesting that this was a way to keep in touch now that he was on the run. Most of the friends got in contact.

So even if you are careful, your friends will blab. There's no technological way around this: so long as someone knows which alias is connected to which real identity, the link may be uncovered. Probably the best we can do is to make sure the link is held by someone who will not open the box to anyone without a warrant. More on this in Chapter 3.

Progress?

The UK government has forced the banks to spend almost a billion pounds on the Current Account Switching System (CASS), reducing the time taken to switch bank accounts from three weeks to one. Yet if I, as a Barclays customer for nearly four decades, decide to go and open an account with Nationwide, I will still have to produce a physical copy of my gas bill and a passport, and they will still have to make photocopies to store. Why can't I just use my very secure Barclays online banking login to log in to Nationwide and open an account? Surely Nationwide trusts Barclays – doesn't it?

We have radio waves and transistors and a nuclear-powered robot trundling around on Mars but we don't have a working identity infrastructure. But before we can say what this infrastructure should be, we need to determine the identity paradigm (in the correct sense of the word: a model of identity) and then develop a narrative around it. John Clippinger writes about the power of identity narratives,[14] and I agree strongly, but we currently lack shared narratives in this area. We need stories to help people understand how identity should work, just as the story of *Star Trek* helped us to understand how communications should work.

Anglo-Saxon attitudes

We think about identity in the wrong way for today. We have a deep-rooted notion of identity that is only tangential to what identity really is now in an online, interconnected, networked nation. This backward-facing and now unhelpful identity paradigm has its roots in the industrial revolution, when we shifted from pre-industrial, local notions of identity to urban anonymity and bureaucracy. As part of this shift, we had to evolve new identity institutions alongside new identity paradigms.

Let me take you back to a time when an English-based international terrorist has been arrested for a murder overseas (using a bomb manufactured in Birmingham), leading to newspaper stories about the activities of a foreign fifth column, based in London but planning assassination worldwide. There ensues a government panic about the ease with which the terrorists are able to travel. This panic becomes linked with more general concerns over the identification of individuals. The British Foreign Secretary announces new rules for identity documents (including a higher price), public anger leads to new legislation being proposed, but the government's bill is defeated and the prime minister resigns.[15] Welcome to 1856. The British government has just launched the passport.

Since Lord Palmerston's government lost that vote, mainly because of public resentment about French pressure fanned by the popular press,[16] we've invented human rights, laser beams, microchips, universal suffrage and the Internet. Yet we have not invented a new version of identity and we (the British) are not at all happy with the old one either. Not all

17

cultures feel the same. If you live anywhere else in Europe, you expect to be able to potter down and open a bank account with an ID card, not with printouts of utility bills, and you do not expect criminals to be able to open mobile phone accounts in your name (for a while the fastest growing category of identity theft in America).

It is certainly the case that these deep-seated attitudes in Britain mean that ID cards have only a 'parasitic vitality'.[17] In other words, they can never take root in the English body politic of their own accord but only by growing on the back of another, much bigger, issue. Thus, it was on the back of that Piedmont anarchist's attempt to murder Emperor Napoleon III and the collapse of the British administration[16] that the passport became the identity document we know today.[15] Up until then passports had been general documents, not even including their carrier's name, and the only way to obtain one had been to know the Foreign Secretary personally. The Earl of Clarendon, Secretary of State for Foreign Affairs at the time, said that the 'British Government attached no importance to passports' (so it is a wonderful irony that the anarchist mentioned above, one Felice Orsini, had in fact travelled to Paris on a passport issued to a Thomas Allsop seven years earlier by Lord Palmerston himself![18]).

Post-industrial passports

Fast-forward to the post-industrial economy, and talk about an 'Internet Passport' is common but profoundly misplaced. Identity in the modern part-mundane, part-virtual world is utterly different to the 'simple' notion of identity rooted in our Victorian concept of passports and identity cards. There is no point in developing an electronic version of a piece of stamped, security-printed paper with a photo and personal information written on it for inspection. I'm not sure any such electronic version is capable of overcoming British or American resistance to identity cards, seen as instruments of state oppression associated only with foreign regimes, a view simply encapsulated in this idea that consistent identification of individuals is a necessary, although not, of course, sufficient precursor to a police state.[19]

Perhaps it is the mental model of identity itself, the essentially Orwellian conception of identity and surveillance that is wrong. Generally speaking, when critics lambast an identity scheme as Orwellian, they are thinking of an omniscient all-controlling state in which perfect surveillance, zero privacy and the total control of information combine to end terrorism, crime and even 'thought crime'. Yet in criticizing schemes on these terms, I think that critics are sharing and propagating the same outdated identity paradigm, a paradigm that is rooted in paper and cardboard, where a person's identity is seen as being singular and fixed, like a card in a card index, rather than multiple and changing; and in which the highly centralized information system that surrounds identity is concerned only with piping related information from the centre to the edge and back again.

As a technologist, I know that technology not even imagined by Orwell writing 1984 in 1948 can deliver far more surveillance than policymakers, civil libertarians, businesses, regulators and legislators realize today. The dangers to both individual liberty and society of 'bad' identity systems are much wider than was apparent to him in 1948 because of that same technology. As the Royal Academy of Engineering's prescient 2007 report on Dilemmas of Privacy and Surveillance noted, we should not be concerned solely with surveillance but also with 'sousveillance'.[20] That is, we should not be concerned only with state snooping and intervention but big business, the press and our next-door neighbours.

The origins of the misleading and simplistic model of identity, the passport model, lie in border control. Today we should be concerned not only with border control between countries and communities but with border control between mundane and virtual communities. Indeed, as Catherine Fieschi of Demos wrote, this mundane–virtual border control may be a good basis for developing modern notions of identity and privacy.[21] One might imagine a flight to virtual communities where mathematics (in the form of cryptography) provides a defence against crime and disorder that the metal barriers of a gated community cannot. If the community decides on a new law, they can enforce it instantly and effectively by excluding transgressors or by persuading them to exclude themselves.[22]

What will the post-industrial replacement for the passport look like? We need an identity infrastructure that admits different kinds of identities, some of which are fixed and some of which are more fluid. We want this infrastructure to deliver appropriate privacy and security. And it goes without saying that society needs this infrastructure to be cost effective; economics is an inescapable discipline.

The economics of privacy are, like anything else, a matter of trade-offs. The problem is that people can't make informed decisions if they don't know exactly what the trade-offs are. It's an imperfect analogy, but consider the case of vehicle safety. Car manufacturers let consumers pick engine size, colour and the fabric on the seats, but not the design of the seat belt. Rather than let people figure out the optimal seat belt for themselves, experts pick a standard. We must be getting close to this point when it comes to identity standards.

The reason is that privacy is important. Privacy permits individuals to express unpopular ideas to people they trust without having to worry about how society will judge them. It is vital to democracy and it contributes to the 'marketplace of ideas' and the promotion of the truth.[23] Privacy, however, is not enough. Private property creates social order and a peaceful society requires a clear allocation of goods and rules for their public use.[24] In other words, as is well known, privacy needs security. So we need security as well.

A privacy paradox

One of the simplest ways to demonstrate both how non-intuitive some aspects of the problem are and also how the use of new technology can deliver new solutions is to consider what I have called the Chatroom Paradox. My kids want to go into chatrooms to discuss everything from computer games to saving the planet. I will only allow them into chatrooms if I know that the other people in the chatrooms aren't serial killers, perverts and so forth. In order to make sure of this, I therefore want the name and address of everybody else in the chatroom so that I can validate them against sex-offenders' registers. However, if somebody else in the chatroom wants my kids' names and address to check them against a register, I don't want to give it to them. What if there's a mistake and they really are a serial killer or pervert? This then is the paradox: in order to harness the power of the Internet, I want full disclosure from everybody else who wants to be part of the subgroup but will refuse any kind of disclosure on my side. Stalemate.

Yet as we technologists will readily point out, through the miracle of public key cryptography, it is straightforward to implement unconditionally unlinkable identities which allow subgroup members to prove to each other that they are over 18, a British citizen, a Manchester City fan, or anything else, without disclosing their identity in a way which could be compromised.

This might also be a way to approach the challenges set out at high level in Hillary Clinton's speech on 'Internet rights and wrongs' back in 2011.[25] She called for (I paraphrase) freedom of communications for people that we like, but not for people that we do not like. It's probably unfair to pick on her about this, because a great many politicians have called for the same thing without having any idea of how it might be achieved.

Such calls demonstrate that it is hard to think about identity and related issues in a networked world using the mental models of the 'old' world. As described here, though, we've been here before. The emergence of the modern passport involved more than the development of new technologies and techniques to document individual identity. It also required a critical rethinking of identification and identity.[26] The result was, it is fair to argue, the emergence of a new identity, one distinct from how people had previously thought of themselves. The emergence of a new passport equivalent will lead, yet again, to a new form of identity, yet again distinct from how we think about ourselves now.

Chapter 3

A new identity for a new world

> The fantastic advances in the field of electronic communications constitute a greater danger to the privacy of the individual.
>
> Earl Warren, 14th Chief Justice of the United States (1963)

It is not going to be easy to develop the next-generation identity infrastructure. One of the main reasons is that we cannot agree on what the underlying model should be. We need to reconstitute a vision of identity for the new world. And we need to begin by recognizing that the technology has changed since Orwell's day, let alone since Napoleon III's, and can deliver far more than the policymakers and public either expect or imagine.

As just noted, to many people in many countries, the idea of a giant database of every single person's singular identity is uncontroversially progress and an essential element of population management. See the case study on Aadhaar on page 26 for a current example. This identity architecture is problematic and would not be right for the UK or the US.

A better architecture distinguishes between identities and the authentication of valid transactions. We need to have very strong authentication against a revocable token (e.g. a smartphone) and use the central database purely for the purposes of eliminating duplicates. Without going into all of the reasons why (OK, here's one: undercover police officers must be able to have two tokens, one for their police identity and one for their undercover identity), this more decentralized option provides simultaneously both more security and more privacy. The central database is there to ensure unique identities, using biometrics for instance, but the authentication of transactions uses the token. When the UK comes (as it inevitably will) to require some kind of 'entitlement card', then I hope it chooses that option.

This is not a pipe dream. In some countries, elements of this new vision are already under construction. In Germany the government has created a system to link identity cards to service-specific virtual identities in order to enhance privacy. In Austria the national identity scheme uses sector-specific identity numbers so the bank can't figure out your police number from your bank number. In Canada, you are identified by an MBUN, a 'meaningless but unique number' (very different from the Swedish identity number which broadcasts your gender and your place and date of birth). In Belgium, citizens can use smartcard readers to access the register themselves and check for mistakes in their own entries. In Finland, citizens can use their identity card to login in via OpenID. In Estonia, the largest mobile operator has issued a SIM card with an identity application on board, a decision that adumbrates the natural transition from card to mobile phone.

These are interesting uses of technology, but they are not by themselves a narrative of the new vision. Too many people still want to use these new technologies in the old context. When he was the British Home Office Minister for ID cards, Andy Burnham said: 'I take the view that it is part of being a good citizen, proving who you are, day in day out.' How wrong can you be? But he is not alone; his successor as Home Office

Minister for ID cards, Meg Hillier, said we should see ID cards as 'passports in-country'. Another Home Office Minister for ID cards before him, Tony McNulty, said: 'There are now so many almost daily occasions when we have to stand up and verify our identity.'

They are all wrong. There are virtually no daily occasions when we have to prove who we are: in general, we are being asked to prove that we are entitled to do something, which is an entirely different issue and one that can be resolved without compromising on privacy. To take the most mundane of examples, my 'identity card' ought to be able to prove to a pub that I am over 18 without telling the pub who I am, which is none of their business (and they can still bar you without knowing your name!).

What is needed to enable transactions is not identity per se but the associated entitlements.

Negative identity

Let's explore what this alternative architecture of entitlements could look like, starting with John Clippinger's notion of 'negative identities'.[14] He defined them as like having a persistent but anonymous identity online: never revealed in full, revealing *just enough to enter into a relationship* (my italics). As he says, the merchant doesn't need to know your name to sell you shoes. Further, he went on to say that 'negative identity should become the default identity online,' a sentiment I strongly agree with.

Rather than 'negative identity', though, I prefer the formulation of '*pseudonyms* with credentials'. As a pseudonym is an identity, a name in the simplest case, which is not your real identity but that is persistent and linked to your real identity. Robert Galbraith was J. K. Rowling's pseudonym for writing

Case Study: Indian National ID

What would it be like to develop a national identity infrastructure from scratch? We have a fascinating case study in India, which is engaged in a gigantic experiment to create a national identity scheme for more than a billion people, from scratch. Called the Aadhaar scheme, it involves giving a 12-digit individual identification number to citizens. The numbers are issued by the UIDAI (Unique Identification Authority of India) and they are stored against the citizen's biometrics. Do they work? *Prospect* magazine had a lovely story in which a chap in Mumbai puts a plastic copy of his wife's fingerprint over his own finger and uses it to fool a biometric reader, thus highlighting some worries about the chosen technology architecture.[27] Nevertheless, the article also notes that the potential benefits to the Indian economy are significant, because businesses of all kinds can use the identity infrastructure to greatly reduce costs.

The market regulator Sebi has said investors can use Aadhaar cards as a valid address proof for their accounts with brokerage firms, mutual funds, portfolio managers and other entities. The card is already permitted as a valid identity proof document in the capital market. Obviously, for this identification scheme to be of most use to business, there must be a way for banks to validate the identification numbers that are presented by customers. This process is going to be automated and the UIDAI is creating software to link the bank directly to the Aadhaar portal.

Given the intimate relationship between social and financial inclusion, one of the most important effects of 'identity inclusion' is that the financially excluded are now given a hand on to the first steps of the financial inclusion 'ladder', as development experts call it. It is wrong to think of this first step as a bank account as we so often do in Europe, because for a great many people the first step is a simple prepaid transaction account. India is already taking the obvious next step to integrate identity and money infrastructures by providing just such transaction accounts that can be linked with the Aadhaar scheme.

The accounts are in the form of a prepaid card, initially available in the National Capital Region (NCR). Indians can take their Aadhaar card and use it to obtain one of these prepaid cards that work rather like the familiar mobile prepaid accounts. They can be topped up in participating banks (at the time of writing these are SBI, ICICI, Axis, HDFC and the Indian Overseas Bank).

Now, there are of course risks in a system that uses a single centralized database. In the fake fingerprint example, the risk is that you can pretend to be someone else. But there's a much bigger risk. Once you can get a fake entry into the database then you are 'behind the wire' so to speak, and your fake identity will never be challenged. This has in fact already happened in the Indian system. There are a variety of ways to get on to the database fraudulently but given any system of this scale, the human factor must come in to play. Since it is not possible to register everyone through the normal channel (e.g. disabled people without fingerprints, people in the witness protection programme, spies and so on) there must be exception channels and these become an attack vector. According to the Indian press, officials have already detected a large number of fraudulent enrolments exploiting the 'biometric exception' clause.

And there's another problem with centralization: it creates a 'honeypot' for personal data which it is worth criminals expending considerable resources to access.

her crime novel *The Cuckoo's Calling*. It was a pseudonym because someone knew that Robert Galbraith was J. K. Rowling, but most people (to start with) did not. A pseudonym can be connected with credentials to form a persona, rather like an avatar in a computer game: not just an identity, but an identity with some attributes.

Pseudonyms are not a mechanism to escape or avoid responsibility. Two-way pseudonymity (between, for example, a person using a chip-and-PIN card to purchase something in a shop and the shopkeeper) makes it possible to arrange anonymity in legal transactions with accompanying legal certainty. This kind of conditional anonymity is socially useful.[28] It has always seemed to me to be the core of the technical architecture that we need to implement identity for the new economy.[29] The idea of persistent pseudonyms as the anchors for relationships is the core of the business processes that will use that architecture.

If identity infrastructures are to serve the needs of our information society, the focus must be moved away from the identities of individuals and become more supportive of pseudonymity,[30] giving people a means to engage in economic and social transactions without having to give away everything about themselves in the process. Another way to express this is, as Jaron Lanier puts it, that people should be able to choose 'economic avatars'.[31]

There's another important point to be made here. We can use pseudonyms to introduce some control over our privacy into the transactional world. Besides, there are some transactions that can only take place in conditions of anonymity (see the case study on adult activities on page 32). Therefore, if we make pseudonyms central to the new identity narrative, we have a solution that is enabling as well as enhancing.

Transactions are not all money

Transactions do not always involve money. Here's a good example: reviews. There's a long-running debate going on about whether people should be able to post online without disclosing their 'real' identity. This is getting especially heated around online review sites such as TripAdvisor.

How do you trust reviews at all?

Reviews are a good thing and one of the best things to emerge from the Internet revolution. You no longer have to depend on anyone's opinion about something because you have access to everyone's. Review sites make a market more transparent and improve the quality of goods and services. Therefore, making the reviews work is important. How do you do this?

If you let people post under assumed names, will they post rubbish? Can you trust a review site where you don't know who anyone is? How will you know whether the reviewers are astroturfing for corporate puppet masters or opening up information for the people? I travel a lot, so I post a lot on TripAdvisor and I use the reviews to choose hotels. But I don't post under my 'real' name as I don't see why who I am is material to a review. My attributes might be material (I'm travelling on business, I don't like spinach, I want somewhere with a gym), but my identity isn't.

Does it matter? It looks as if it doesn't. In fact, insofar as there is any evidence, it is that pseudonymous interaction online is actually better than either identifiable or anonymous interaction. Disqus, the well-known online comment management platform used by many news organizations, says that not only does allowing pseudonyms produce more comments, but the quality of the comments is also better, as measured by likes and replies. In short, people who use pseudonyms post better comments on Disqus.[32] Their comments are liked more and generate more discussion. I can think of many reasons why this is true (one of the main ones being that people reveal their real likes and dislikes, prejudices and opinions, views and perspectives under pseudonyms, whereas they are always constrained when using their 'real' names) and it certainly matches with my experiences in online chat and debate environments.

Personally, whether it's posting abusive messages about government ministers or arguing about the merits of a return to the gold standard, I always use pseudonyms unless I am posting in a professional capacity, in which case (I sincerely hope) my expertise and experience are relevant to the discussion at hand. In some cases I use the same pseudonym across multiple sites; in other cases I use a specific pseudonym.

In the case of reviews, though, how do you know the reviewer stayed in the hotel or took the flight or ate in the restaurant? One way would be to institute a system of cryptographic tokens so that the customer can only post a review of something if they have a token showing that they used it; and it should take a court order for the token provider to reveal the person who had the token.

The service would work something like this: when you pay at the hotel, your electronic wallet generates a token that the hotel chain digitally signs and sends back. The hotel doesn't know who this token is going to, only that it is going to someone who really did stay in the hotel. To write a review, you must submit the token. The review site can easily check the digital signature from the hotel chain that proves that you did stay at the hotel during the previous month (or whenever) but it doesn't link to your identity. The hotel can be sure that you were a customer, but neither they nor the review service know who you are. If you post something that is against the law, a court can then order the service to turn over the connection.

Technology has a solution here to a real problem. It would be easy for a US newspaper, say, to require commenters to have a digital identity from a US provider. These digital identities should be pseudonymous as a default: thus, I can post political comment or hotel reviews or jokes about celebrities or whatever. If I actually libel someone (under sensible libel laws, not the UK's libel laws), then someone can get a court order to ask the identity provider to reveal the digital identity that they were provided with (this, of course, may in some circumstances be another pseudonym).

There are many different organizations that might be prepared to provide a useful pseudonym: let's say my mobile operator gave me the identity 'dinosaurdave'. I go around logging in to various websites as dinosaurdave using the mobile handset as part of a two-factor authentication (2FA) process (like the one available for logging securely into Facebook, for example). Now suppose I log in somewhere and post a libel. The target goes to court and gets an order: this is delivered to O2 (digitally signed by the Attorney General, naturally) and O2 will then return my name and billing address. Without the court order, cryptography means that no one can find out who dinosaurdave is. This seems like a reasonable accommodation.

A final point. For pseudonyms to have a value, they need to be underwritten by trusted institutions. If I come to your site presenting a pseudonym that is underwritten by my bank (so that you know that my bank knows who I am), then you will be comfortable allowing me in even though you don't know who

Case Study: Adult Activities

For reasons too complicated to go into, I found myself investigating the payment mechanisms used in the provision of adult services online and ended up talking to women who provide webcam services on the Internet. It was a small and unscientific survey, but by far the most common form of payment that I came across was gift certificates.

I had a nice chat with a lady called Carole from Indiana, who explained that, for her, Amazon gift certificates are quick and convenient. Amazon's scale means that their gift certificates are a liquid asset that trades at par. (It wouldn't bother me to have part of my salary paid as Amazon gift certificates since I spend a fortune there.) Around a third of US consumers have a credit card on file with Amazon and since most of Carole's customers were American they almost all had Amazon accounts; and if they didn't it took five minutes to set one up using a webmail address.

Amazon wasn't the only option, by the way, but it was certainly a common one. Here's a typical set of 'payment instructions' from another woman's website:

> Amazon egift card – Amazon offers almost everything. One of my favorite online stores; Victoria's Secret egift card. I am a regular; Agent Provocateur evoucher – I am so addicted to it.

Here is how an Amazon transaction works. Carole's customer logs in as 'XXX@hotmail.com' (for example) and sends a gift certificate to her at 'YYY@hotmail.com'. (I made these up – I sincerely apologize if they are real email addresses.) It arrives in a couple of seconds. Transaction complete. He never knows her real name, she never knows his real name, but a trusted intermediary makes the transaction happen. Carole clicks on the egift certificate and it is immediately credited to her account.

Note the identity flow. The customer uses their credit card in their own name, but Carole never sees that. The value is credited to Carole's account with her real identity, but the customer never sees that. There is two-sided conditional anonymity: neither party knows who their counterparty really is, but they know that Amazon does and that's enough to enable the transaction. The anonymity is conditional because obviously if the police turned up with a warrant and asked Amazon for 'Carole's' details, the anonymity would be broken.

(As an aside, on 16 April 2013, some time after I wrote the original notes for this case study, Amazon was granted US Patent no. 8,423,457 'Anonymous Mobile Payments' for 'A computer-implemented method of providing an anonymous mobile payment to enable transfer of an electronic payment between a provider and a recipient without an exchange of personal information between the provider and the recipient...'.)

Carole explained that she only works mornings because she has stuff to do in the afternoons, and that since she does all of her online shopping with Amazon anyway, it's pretty convenient to stack up the gift certificates and then order stuff and that it saves her time going out shopping too. At this point, I made my excuses and left.

I am because if anything goes wrong you can always ask the bank. If I present a pseudonym that is underwritten by someone you've never heard of (or perhaps even me), it might not be acceptable in some cases but acceptable in others.

The issue of pseudonyms, the Clinton paradox and the distinction between entitlement and identification give us a much better guide for a new identity architecture, with privacy-enhancing technologies (PETs) at their heart, than something like the centralized Indian Aadhaar scheme (page 26). To go back to the Chatroom Paradox, imagine a situation where my kids log in using a digital certificate provided by, let's say, Barclays Bank. Perhaps there's a USB contactless card reader attached to their PC or the chatroom can access something provided by the bank in the kids' mobile phones. They log in and up pops a menu, 'Who do you want to be?' followed by a list of identities, each of which is actually a digital certificate stored on the bank card or in the phone. My son chooses 'L33t 6gun' or whatever, and punches in his PIN. The certificate containing the L33t 6gun identity – digitally signed by Barclays Bank as a service to Premier Customers – is sent off to the server. Let's say it's a BBC chatroom.

The certificate contains data that allows the BBC to determine that my son is actually between the ages of 11 and 16 – through some mathematical magic known as an interval proof – but nothing else. Thus, the BBC knows nothing about my son's actual identity: all they have received is the certificate testifying to his age. But now suppose that one of the kids does something they shouldn't do – posts a bomb-making manual or goes browsing a knife catalogue. Then the police can go to the BBC and ask for the certificate. They know it must really have come from the Barclays Bank because the certificate carries – thanks to some mathematical magic known as *asymmetric cryptography* – an unforgeable digital signature from Barclays Bank. The police can then ask Barclays Bank whom the certificate was issued to. And Barclays Bank, being a law-abiding and responsible organization, will tell them. There's no need for Big Brother: in this vision, my child's identity is only revealed if they misbehave and stays hidden otherwise. To me, this seems a much better rebalancing of the relationship between citizen and state.

Next imagine that the perception of the government, businesses and citizens is amended to see the identity management as a utility, available to everyone. Then the national identity management scheme could become a form of public utility, regulated by the government (but not necessarily delivered by it, except for the core 'gold standard' national record[33]). This national record need comprise nothing more than a unique number and the associated biometrics. There is no need to store anything else (such as names) because the national record has a simple, clear, attainable purpose: to ensure the uniqueness of the underlying national ID number. That's it.

A simple extension to this idea of MBUNs and biometrics might be to use sector-specific identifiers as in the Austrian example, so that the 'police number' is not the same as the 'bank number', which is not the same as the 'health number' for example. This stops the casual trawling of databases that can so easily undermine public confidence. A 'privacy broker' ensures that when someone queries the database, they get back the correct number. If you were to be carried unconscious into a hospital, the hospital could in principle send off your fingerprints and get back your health number. If you were to be carried unconscious into a police station, the police could in principle send off your fingerprints and get back your police number. The police would have to obtain a warrant to ask the privacy broker for your health number, which seems a reasonable restriction to me. The German ID card had a similar reasonable compromise proposed: one 'number' for police and border control, another 'number' for e-government and e-business.[34]

In this architecture, just as the national record has a simple clear purpose, so does this kind of national identity scheme. The purpose of the scheme is to deliver privacy. That is its narrative.

35

The identity card, the identity application in the smartphone, the identity 'software as a service' (SaaS), are all different manifestations of the privacy broker I described above.

If it's a pub asking, all the broker will tell it is whether you are over 18 or not. If it's a hospital asking, all the card will tell it is your health number, and so on. What's more, cryptographic techniques mean that the individual's privacy is protected by well-understood cryptographic algorithms rather than by the good intentions of the providers and their staff and contractors, or by the strictures of an ombudsman.

From one, many

Let's take it as read that we can build a national infrastructure along these lines. What would we do with it? If we could manage several identities simply and effectively using our mobile phones as a kind of remote control, for example, why would we restrict ourselves to a single identity?

The British Government's Chief Scientist, Professor Sir John Beddington, published a Foresight report on identity (which says, interestingly, that 'the UK is now a virtual environment as well as a real place')[35] in which he emphasized the plural nature of identity in the modern world. He said:

> 'identity' is not a simple notion. People can have many different overlapping identities which are fundamental to their individuality. Identities can exercise a powerful influence on the health and wellbeing of communities, and the degree to which they can build up social capital. There are important implications for a range of policy issues...

He also talked about balancing privacy and security, a formulation I am uncomfortable with because it should be government policy to increase both (more on this below). His point about different and overlapping identities is, though, central to the construction of an identity narrative that fits the world evolving around us. Aleks Krotoski put this very well[36] when she observed the relationship between identity and community, echoing the Disqus findings about the quality of interaction involving persistent pseudonyms:

> Most interesting are the accounts I have on other networks that are totally unrelated to my 'Aleks Krotoski' identity. They're not anonymous to the people in those communities: I've been an active member posting under the same pseudonym for a decade , and the people there know me under that identity.

It is not simply that we have multiple identities and that we are learning how to exist in a fragmented identity environment. When speaking at 'The Life of Mobile Data' at the University of Surrey back in 2004, Charles Raab (Professor at the AHRB Research Centre in Intellectual Property and Technology, School of Law, University of Edinburgh) said that

> In the world of post-modernism, it is no longer clear that any one identity is 'real'.

This is one of the most insightful comments I ever heard on the topic, and one that continues to have a profound impact on my thinking. The breakthrough that we need to make to complete our narrative is to drop the idea that any one of our identities is automatically privileged. *All* of the identities we exchange are virtual, and while these virtual identities are of course linked to our mundane identities, they should not be confused. None of them is 'real'.

But what does this mean and why is it the key to developing the new vision called for in the previous section? How can society deal with multiple identities?

Here's a practical and immediate example. The British government has announced that it is to reform the Witness Protection Scheme (WPS), which, as the name suggests, protects people who have given evidence in criminal trials. The people and their families are given new identities and moved to another part of the country to start a new life. There are currently 3,000 people under protection in this way.

Witness protection is one of those cases that makes the design of an identity system interesting and complex. During my time in 2008 as a member of the Home Office Advisory Forum in the days of the proposed UK national identity card, witness protection was one of the factors that persuaded me that a token-based solution was the way forward, rather than some form of purely biometric, centralized solution (such as the Indian model discussed earlier).

There's a great danger in accepting an infrastructure of passive identification where you, the target, do not have a choice in how you are identified. It may seem superficially attractive to have centralized solutions that do not require tokens, but I really don't want websites to identify me every time I visit them. This is not because I'm in the WPS but because I want a very basic choice of interacting as Dave Birch the private citizen or Dave Birch the executive officer of Consult Hyperion or John Doe.

In such a system, how does the identity infrastructure know which identity to use? I suppose one way of determining this would be to look at the nature of the request. Imagine a national identity service that was solely based on personal characteristics. It doesn't matter whether they are your fingerprint, face, typing pattern or anything else. The chap at the pub wants to know whether you are 18 or not, so he captures the relevant characteristic (let's use fingerprints for the purposes of discussion) and fires it off to the identity service.

The identity service sees that your fingerprints appear twice in the record: once for your 'real' identity and once for your 'witness' identity. Since it is a pub asking, the service sends back your witness identity and life goes on. But, for example, if it is a policeman asking, then the system might return both identities. This would of course be insanely dangerous because, as is well documented, unauthorized access by policemen and others to existing databases is rampant and it will be no trouble for criminals to determine a person's other identities. In the case of the ill-fated UK national identity card, unauthorized access to the identity database started before the system ever went live, and both central and local government workers were fired.

It's one thing to have trusted and vetted and responsible officials rummaging around in a National Identity Database, but imagine what happens when just about anyone gets access to that database and it is recording who is in the WPS. Actually, you don't have to imagine that because we already know. The BBC indicated in a 2009 article that, according to a report by a Mexican magistrate, [translation] 'the majority of protected witnesses who have cooperated with the judicial system in Mexico have been assassinated'.[37]

If you are a spy, or an undercover policeman, or in the WPS, or perhaps even a restaurant critic, you may have perfectly legitimate reasons (in some cases very literally a matter of life and death) for wanting one identity declared rather than another. Who controls this? In a token-based environment, there is no problem. A policeman stops me in the street and wants to know who I am. I take out my phone and touch it against his phone. His phone requests an authenticated identity, my phone asks me for a PIN or pass code, which I enter, and my phone sends back my driving licence, which includes a photograph that is displayed on the policeman's phone. In this latter case, my personal characteristics might form part of the process but only for the purposes of local authentication against the token: thus I might be required to speak into my phone or present my fingerprint to the phone, for example, but this would be used only within the phone for template matching.

No one is real

An identity service founded on the principles that apply online thus has no problem dealing with multiple identities. In essence, it treats all identities as pseudonyms. The use of the pseudonym that happened to coincide with your 'real' name would not be a special case. To see what I mean, imagine that my name is Jelly Dave (an epithet earned through my knowledge and skill in using gelignite to open safes). I fall out with Mr Big, the head of my gang of bank robbers, and I decide to turn Queen's Evidence and start a new life. Quite straightforward: my identity is revoked and I'm given a new one. I use that digital identity to obtain a new pseudonym from the national identity service (in essence, I send them my blinded public key, they send me back a signed public key certificate and then I remove the blinding) and I'm now Telly Dave, a couch potato from Woking. If a policeman stops me in the street, my phone tells him that I'm Telly Dave. If he is corrupt, it doesn't matter, because there is no link between Telly Dave and Jelly Dave. The pub, the policeman and everyone else are provided with a pseudonym, not the underlying real identity. Since neither the pub nor the policeman has access to the biometric register that ensures uniqueness, they never see the MBUN that connects the pseudonym to the physical entity.

Incidentally, the witness protection issue is about to get substantially more complex. Using digital identity infrastructure it is easy to give you a new pseudonym, but it is not easy to give you a new social graph. Witness protection in the age of Facebook is a whole lot more complicated because protecting your privacy in an online age is a minefield, as Facebook founder Mark Zuckerberg's sister rather famously discovered when a photograph that she took spread around the web because she hadn't set the Facebook privacy settings correctly.

My new identity of Telly Dave is sooner or later going to get tagged in a photo somewhere that will end up with Mr Big. So without knowing anything about the WPS itself, or how the government proposes to restructure it, I would think that it has a massive job on its hands to set about forging the social graph for spies, undercover policeman, protected witnesses and restaurant critics in the face of services like Trulioo, which helps to uncover phoney Facebook identities.

Anti-social networking

In short, the future of identity isn't about creating an electronic version of the passport and finding a way to bind people to that one identity at all times via a big – and vulnerable – database. The future of identity is much richer and more complex.

Your identity of the future is a network-based, socially supported pseudonym. With judicious use of the PETs discussed above, identity can work online in an acceptable way that simultaneously provides more security and more privacy. (They are related, of course: you cannot have privacy without security, although security without privacy is no problem at all.)

This kind of identity makes sense in terms of the technology we have, the business structures that work and the needs of people and organizations. It delivers privacy infrastructure that meets the real demands of society as whole. Human rights law already requires that everyone should have their reasonable expectation of privacy respected and protected.

Article 20 of the Universal Declaration of Human Rights protects the right to freedom of peaceful assembly and association. In the US, the First Amendment to the Constitution similarly protects freedom of association.

But is the legal guarantee of privacy still realistic?[38] Clarification of what counts as a reasonable expectation of privacy is necessary in order to protect this right and, as that Royal Academy of Engineering working group (of which I was a member) said back in 2007, a public debate, including the legal, technical and political communities, must be encouraged in order to work towards a consensus on the definition of what is a 'reasonable expectation'. This debate should take into account the effect of an easily searchable Internet when deciding what counts as a reasonable expectation of privacy.[20] In a post-PRISM world (something we know about thanks to the revelations by Edward Snowden), the need for this informed debate is greater than ever and extends well beyond the possibilities afforded by this text. I would like to suggest, however, that the essence of privacy in a networked world is personal control. A very practical way to control who can interact with you, your credentials and your reputation is to partition 'you' into the multiple personas formed from pseudonyms. This may seem odd to those born before the web, but the web generation have a different view of identity (see the case study on page 45), a view of identity informed by social networking.

Whereas social networking links your complete identity with other people's complete identities, 'anti-social' networking links one persona to another persona. It's a better form of online community because it enables participants to choose which facets of their personalities they want to present to others. This gives people the opportunity to create, destroy and remake their online personas. It is in sympathy with the

American ethos of optimism, pragmatism and self-help[39] and a practical mechanism to resolve many paradoxes of online life.

Offline it is a different issue of course and it isn't really the focus of this discussion, but I think it probably is worth making the point that we may be heading into an era where online privacy will be part of the infrastructure of interaction and therefore maintained and managed properly, whereas offline privacy will degenerate to the point of invisibility. One does not have to be entirely paranoid about the combination of CCTV, personal drones and face-recognition technology to realize the privacy in its current form is ending. In the emerging online privacy-managed space, however, things can be different. We can start from first principles to imagine how privacy should work and then we can implement it using a combination of the technologies discussed so far. Of course, for all of this to work properly, there has to be some kind of framework in place for the identities of the future to interact.

Identity frameworks

The subject of the Visa Europe Research Fellowship at the Centre for the Study of Financial Innovation (CSFI) for 2011/12 was 'Identity and Financial Services'; and the goal was to find a way to make an order-of-magnitude reduction in financial-sector transaction costs by dealing with the proliferation of usernames and passwords, dongles and devices that form the current piecemeal approach to the 'identity problem'. I was the research fellow for this project, which was based on the CSFI's tried and tested roundtable formula, with representatives of organizations from around Europe, ranging from banks and mobile operators to governments and independent experts. It proved simultaneously fascinating and frustrating. Fascinating because each of the roundtables revealed new perspectives on the problem and frustrating because these perspectives widened as the research evolved. From the apparently simple questions at the beginning (such as, why can't I use my dongle from Bank A to create an account at Bank B? Why can't I use my highly secure chip-and-PIN card to get access to DVLA or HMRC?) to the apparently simple questions at the end (what is identity anyway?) a wide range of problems, solutions and opportunities was presented and debated.

To simplify grossly, three basic models for identity services emerged. We might label these, for ease of reference, the Scandinavian, Continental and Atlantic models. The Scandinavian model is one of banks providing identities that are used by business and government; the Continental model is of government identities that are used by banks and business; and the Atlantic model is of banks and business providing identities that are used by each other and by government.

I think that there is much to be commended in the Atlantic model, adopted in the US under the banner of the National Strategy for Trusted Identities in Cyberspace (NSTIC) and in the UK under the banner of the Cabinet Office–led Identity Assurance Programme (IDA). This model could, in principle, cope with a spectrum of identity and privacy paradigms from Canada to China. The idea is a framework for public/private acceptance of federated identities and in both cases the private sector would be providing those identities. I'm very much in favour of this model: if I choose to use my Barclays identity to access the DVLA, or my DWP identity to access O2, it shouldn't matter to the effective and efficient use of online transactions. Given that these initiatives have identified the right direction of travel, discussion and debate around them has been poor at best and a caricature at worst. In the

Case Study: Cheering for Social Media

Social media puts into sharp relief the differences between the adult view of identity and the emerging Generation Y (or Generation Whatever, as they are known in our household) view of identity. A lawsuit filed in the US illustrates this rather well. The suit alleged that a school teacher, in her capacity as a cheerleading coach, demanded that members of her squad hand over their Facebook login information. According to the suit, the teacher used it to access a student's account, which included a heated discussion of some of the cheerleading squad's internal politics. That information was then shared widely among school administrators, which resulted in the student receiving various sanctions.

What I found fascinating about this story is the lesson it contains about emerging norms around identity in a digital age. Look at the reaction of some of the other kids who were faced with the same demand. The teacher and the students could not actually log in to Facebook because the school had a filter that blocked it. So the kids used their mobile phones to log in and delete their Facebook accounts.

The kids aren't stupid: they live in that world and they can distinguish their multiple virtual identities. Faced with a privacy violation that undermines a virtual identity, they slash and burn. And the school's efforts to prevent them manipulating their virtual identities are fruitless.

I therefore regard this as an uplifting story: we might not yet understand exactly what we mean by privacy in the Facebook age, and we may be aghast at what kids post on their pages, but we can at least see that they do have a sense of what is right and wrong in that unfamiliar world.

> What's more, they have an understanding of the tools so that they can take some control over what is happening out on the wild frontier. A natural teenage response: I'm sure my kids would sooner delete their Facebook accounts than give me their passwords. Not just because there might be embarrassing stuff there, but because they feel that the Facebook identity, while just a persona, has an integrity that is destroyed once someone else has the password.

US, news outlets reported NSTIC as a new law that requires American citizens to hold an Internet ID card! No one will have to have an 'Internet Driver's License' (note, by the way, that there are those who think this would be a good idea) but they will be able to log in to their bank, the government, the actual driving licence authorities and their favourite blogs using a variety of IDs provided by their bank, their mobile phone operator and others.

So how would it work? In essence, you would have three or four identities given to you by different Identity Providers (IDPs) much as you have three or four cards given to you by different banks at the moment. In the UK, there are currently eight such providers approved by the government, including PayPal, the Post Office and Experian. You might have a bank identity, a hobby identity, an education identity and a travel identity, for example.

Each of these identities may have attached to it one or more attributes that come from a variety of Attribute Providers (APs). The Royal Mail might be the preferred provider of the 'address' attribute. My bank identity and my travel identity might both use this same attribute. An identity and one or more attributes are bound together in digital certificates, and it is these certificates that are passed around to support transactions.

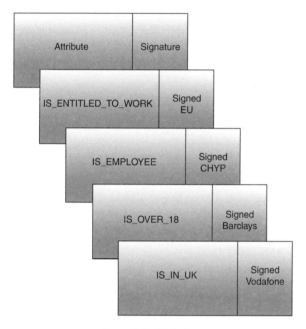

Figure 3.1. Attributes.

If I want to know your age, and you present a certificate that contains an identity that I can understand and verify together with an age attribute (that you are over 18, say) that comes from a provider that I recognize and trust, and all of this can be checked automatically, then you have what is called a 'credential'. In this case, I'll label the credential IS_OVER_18.

Credentials

To understand how these frameworks would be used in practice, I need to introduce the notions of a public-key certificate (PKC) and a public-key infrastructure (PKI), which are central to much of modern Internet cryptography. Now is not the time to explain how public-key cryptography works (it's all about prime numbers and such like), but I do need to explain what a certificate is so that you can see how credentials work.

A PKC is an identity and one or more attributes, with some other information (such as an expiry date) that are put together and digitally signed by a third party. The attributes might come from a variety of sources, as shown in Figure 3.1. If you send me such a certificate, I can use the PKI to check the digital signatures so I can trust the contents. If Barclays tell me that you are a UK resident, over 18 and with good credit, then I'm happy to trust that.

A note on expiration dates. These provide a safety net. A bad credential can be out there for only so long. We can imagine a credential in an application where fraud is rampant that would expire every week, every day or every hour. It would be a pain to deal with this in the pen-and-paper world, but it works just fine in cyberspace.[40]

We need standards for credentials and such like so that I can use my Woking Council ID to log in to central government services and my Barclays Bank ID to log in to do my taxes online. There are good business reasons for going down this route. I can imagine that Barclays might provide a basic identity (that would enable me to log in to my bank account, or open an account at another bank) but I might pay Barclays for an additional ID that has some key credentials (IS_A_PERSON, IS_OVER_18, IS_NOT_BANKRUPT) but that does not reveal my identity. This sort of Joe Bloggs (or, for our cousins over the water, John Doe) identity would be more than adequate for the vast majority of web browsing and if other people want to wander the highways and byways of the Internet with a Manchester United, Prince or BBC ID, then it's up to them. Let a thousand flowers bloom.

Only connect

Now, in the absence of some kind of mandatory government e-ID, while there may be the potential for a thousand flowers to bloom, there are at present just one or two sunflowers already poking their faces over the fence. Facebook Connect lets any website on the planet use its infrastructure for identification and authentication. It's easy to implement, just a few lines of code on a web server. Once installed, visitors see a 'Log in with Facebook' button. If they're already logged into Facebook they can just click and get in, otherwise they will be redirected to Facebook to log in with their user name and password and then bounced back to the site. I'm sure most people reading this will have used Facebook or Twitter or Google or similar to log in somewhere. I do it all the time: in fact, I have a couple of Facebook accounts in different names that I use only for this purpose as it's a very convenient way of 'grouping' online behaviour, a crude proxy for the multiple identities that should be available.

Like many people, I imagine, I already engage in simplistic persona management using social network identity. If I'm logging in to some work-related website, then I'll probably use my LinkedIn identity. In other cases, I'll use my Twitter identity. I use my Google identity for a bunch of other services. But should other people use those identities? Should potential employers look at potential employees' Facebook pages (to take the obvious case)? I tend not to use Facebook Connect too much because websites that use it often want access to your social graph and other information and by and large I don't feel comfortable with that. I am clearly in a minority though.

In the absence of frameworks defined by governments, there is no doubt that these emergent identity infrastructures will grow anyway because of social media. This may have unexpected ramifications, because the way that people regard their social media identities has no conventional analogue. At the moment most of these log-ins use a password, perhaps with a fiddly sort-of secure 2FA using mobile phones. When I log in to PayPal, for example, it sends a security code to my mobile phone and I have to type this in to get in to my account. The idea is that an attacker would have to steal my phone (hard) as well as my password (easy) in order to misdirect my money. Apple have just launched a similar system for access to their iCloud services.

When I log in to my bank account, however, a much stronger form of 2FA is used. I am with Barclays, and I have to use either my phone or a small plastic calculator-type device to provide an eight-digit passcode when I log in. To be honest, this works pretty well. When they first sent me the device I thought it might get annoying, but I got used to it pretty quickly and now find it easy and reassuring.

Widespread 2FA access to online services really should have become a business for banks or mobile operators already (think how long Identrust has been around) but it just hasn't happened: I can't use my Barclays PINsentry to log on to Barclaycard, let alone the government or an insurance company. But suppose my Facebook Connect account required access to my mobile phone to provide 2FA but that it was a stronger form of authentication than an SMS code (as these can be intercepted). It's straightforward to see how this might work. You have a Facebook app on your phone: when you try to log in to Facebook the app on the phone pops up and asks for a PIN, and once you've entered the PIN then the website, mobile site, TV site or whatever else it was you were trying to log in to with Facebook is there for you.

Case Study: ID in British Columbia

The BC Services Card lays the foundation for changing the way BC citizens interact with their government. In 2011, the government of BC set out to develop a smartcard credential and associated identity information management system, issue the cards to BC citizens and enable access to government services using the cards and identity information services. Starting this year, most adults will obtain their card when renewing their BC driver's licence, which involves an in-person visit to a driver licensing office. As the BC Ministry of Technology, Innovation and Citizen Services (MTICS) put it, it will enable citizens:

> To access a wide range of government services in-person and online, all with one privacy-respecting secure card.

The BC Services Card Program is an integrated programme between the Ministry of Health, the Insurance Corporation of British Columbia (ICBC) and MTICS. This partnership was created in order to leverage the respective strengths and mandates of each organization. The Ministry of Health administers the Medical Services Plan (MSP), in which almost all BC residents are enrolled, and has the most comprehensive client base of all public sector programmes. ICBC provides province-wide infrastructure, technology and best practices for in-person identity proofing and card issuance.

The card, which thus replaces the driver's licence, the health card (each BC resident enrolled with the MSP is eligible for a BC Services Card with a unique lifetime personal health number) and photo ID, has a microchip on board and a contactless interface. Unlike the cards it is replacing, it is also designed to be used online.

The province has a six-year deal with Toronto-based SecureKey to provide card-reader technology to develop BC card readers. These are tiny, key-sized devices that plug into a computer's USB port and have a contactless reader built in. People tap their new CareCard or Services Card onto the SecureKey reader and enter a PIN on a government website to authenticate their identity.

Since all the citizen has to do is to tap their card against the reader, the same ease of use as an Oyster card in London or a Clipper card in San Francisco, this is a simple way to obtain better security with easy access.

Under the hood, there's some serious cryptography at work. It would mean that I could use Facebook Connect for serious business. This would have an interesting side effect: Facebook would know where I go on the web and this would give them tremendous knowledge that could be used for commercial purposes. It's not that Facebook is especially clever (or especially evil), it's just that in a social media world there's an inevitable agglomeration of power attendant on identity provision. Facebook has more than a billion users and is the second most-used smartphone app in the world so they are a natural choice of social media identity provider for a great many people.

The analysts Gartner say that within two years half of new retail customer identities will be based on social network identities, up from less than one in twenty today. Clearly consumers are happy to use their social network identities in this way but I should imagine that some businesses might be uncomfortable with giving Facebook information (which, as we all know, is power) about their customers and what they want to buy.

Horizons

Whether you would prefer some kind of centralized government national identity infrastructure or a world of competing corporate identities, it is clear that the new identity infrastructure is evolving. The implications of this new kind of identity infrastructure are so great as to be almost overwhelming. The way we think about identity, the way we use identity, the way that we manage identity: we are at cultural cusp and there is no going back. Going forward, identity is going to be vastly different.

Now, a great many things are going to change because of this. Community, crime and commerce will be as different to us a generation from now as their pre-industrial revolution versions are to us now (and each of those examples deserves a book of its own) but in this book I explore only one of the areas about to be utterly transformed. Let's talk about money.

Chapter 4

Imagine there's no money

'He had his cash money, but you couldn't pay for food with that. It wasn't actually illegal to have the stuff, it was just that nobody ever did anything legitimate with it.'

William Gibson in *Count Zero*

The key to understanding the effect of technological change on money is to understand the relationship between the functions of money and the technology drivers, because those drivers affect the different functions in different ways and across different timescales.

Tallies and technologies

This relationship is illustrated perfectly by the wonderful story of the tallies, the wooden sticks used to record taxes due to the Crown in England. They first came into use shortly after the Norman invasion of 1066. Tax assessments were made for areas of the country and the sheriff (the shire reeve) was required to collect the tax due and hand it over to the Crown. To ensure that both the sheriff and the king knew where they stood, the tax assessment was recorded by cutting notches in a wooden stick. The stick was then split into two pieces, a larger 'stock' and a smaller 'foil', so that both parties had a durable record of the assessment. When it was time to 'tally up', the sheriff would show up with the tax due and his foil to be matched against the king's stock. The new technology worked well. The sticks were small and long lasting (very long lasting, in fact, given that they still exist), were easy to store and transport, and were easily understood by an illiterate population.

The technology soon began to exhibit unforeseen (in the context of their record-keeping function) characteristics. This is generally true of all technologies and one of the main reasons for this is their persistence. There is no overnight change. As the historian David Edgerton wrote in his detailed study of the phenomenon of technological change, *The Shock of the Old*, it takes a very long time for technologies to move through a culture, and their downstream use is often different to that imagined by their inventors. Money is no different. As he says, 'The modern world is a world of "creole" technologies, technologies transplanted from their origins to find use of a greater scale elsewhere',[41] and this will certainly be true of the technologies that replace cash.

Back in medieval times the king couldn't be bothered to wait until taxes fell due and wanted cash as soon as possible for all sorts of reasons. The king could not borrow money at interest against the collateral of a stock, because of the religious injunction against usury, so he would instead sell the stock at a discount. The holder of the stock could then get the cash when the taxes fell due. This made the stock (in effect) a fixed-term government bond. Selling stocks at a discount became a key means for the Crown to borrow money without God noticing what was going on.

There was an immediate result of this shift in function from a record-keeping to transactional technology: the value of an individual tally was no longer fixed by the amount of tax it entitled the holder to, but by the market, and the market evolved quickly. Someone in (say) Bristol who was holding a stock for taxes due in (say) York would either have to travel to collect their due payment or find someone else who would, for an appropriate discount, buy it. Thus, a market for tallies grew, arbitrating temporal and spatial preferences by discounting, transferring economic resources across space and time before the pre-modern banking system began to emerge to implement these functions. London money markets are not new! The efficiency of this market helped the Crown to raise money more cost-effectively than it might otherwise have done and it is known from recorded instances that officials working in the Exchequer helped this secondary market to operate smoothly.[42]

Incidentally, the tallies remained in use until the nineteenth century. When the last person who knew how to carve tally sticks died in 1826, they were stacked in a corner and forgotten until 1834, when the Treasury had ordered the underused tally office in the Exchequer's room in the Palace of Westminster to be cleared out to make way for the new bankruptcy court. John Phipps, the Assistant Surveyor for London in the Office of Woods and Forests, and, for the usual strange English historical reasons, in charge of the Palace, told the clerk of works at the Palace, Richard Weobley, to take them out and burn them next to the River Thames. Weobley came up with a better idea, which was that they should be burnt in the furnaces that formed part of the 'central heating' system.[43] The tallies were duly loaded into the furnaces and burned very well, resulting in the famous fire that destroyed the medieval palace on 16 October 1834.

Thus, the technology of money, like all technologies, exhibits the law of unintended consequences, so beware of anyone who claims that they can see clearly the direction in which a new technology will take us. The tallies began as a technology for record-keeping, soon went on to become the basis of a money market, and then remained in use long after 'better' alternatives were available. It's impossible to say what the unintended consequences of current innovations in financial technology will be, only to observe that there will be some.

What we see today, with chip cards and the Internet and mobile phones coming together to change the nature of money, is nothing new. Society has been through times of innovation in money technology with considerable long-term ramifications before. In England at the end of the seventeenth century there was a crisis in the means of exchange because of coin 'clipping' with the result that people wouldn't take silver coins in payment nor bring them to the mint for replacement. No less a brain than Isaac Newton (a reasonable candidate for the title of cleverest person ever) quickly figured out what to do.

First, he suggested, the mint should use machines instead of people to make coins. This would vastly reduce the cost of production (and therefore increase mint profits) and would also introduce uniformity and consistency to the coinage. Second, he suggested that the machines 'mill' the edge of the coins to prevent further clipping. The king himself agreed to these changes, with his proclamation of 19 December 1695, referring to 'the great mischiefs which this our kingdom lies under, by reason that the coin, which passes in Payment, is generally clipped'.

Newton's conclusions were correct (to match an industrializing economy to industrial production of money) but it still took a generation (30 years, in fact) to replace the old, clipped, hand-made coins with shiny new emblems of the nascent industrial revolution. If these advances in coinage took time, things didn't accelerate with paper. The earliest UK cheque recognizable in its modern form dates from 1659: it instructs a London goldsmith to pay £400 to a certain Mr Delboe. It took more than a century after cheques were invented for cheque clearing to be invented, and it wasn't invented by banks but by their clerks. Tired of running round to every bank to clear cheques, they began to meet (unofficially) at a coffee house to clear and settle between themselves. (Some years later the banks realized their clerks' idea was a good one and in 1833 established a clearing house at 10 Lombard Street.)

By the time Newton died in 1727, a generation after the currency crisis that had led to his appointment, Britain had a central bank (the Bank of England), banknotes in wide circulation, a working coinage and a gold standard. At the time of the Glorious Revolution of 1688, none of these had existed, yet within a generation money had changed completely. The world of bullion and coins had been replaced by a world of paper and signatures.

We are at an analogous point in the co-evolving relationship between the technology and the money.

Cash is a hack

At the 2013 South-by-Southwest Interactive conference (SXSW) in Austin, Texas, there was a session called 'Identity + 30' run by Sam Lessin, the Head of the Identity Product Group at Facebook. He argued that when sharing is expensive, or when it makes an individual less well-off, people don't share. I won't give you my spare bread if I don't get anything in return or if it costs me more to swap my bread for your chicken than it benefits me. Human societies evolved trade to deal with the costs of exchange, and we evolved trust networks to do it efficiently by growing larger networks with more trading

Case Study: PayPal in Physical Commerce

PayPal grew to be a major player in the electronic payment world by providing a convenient means of sending money from person to person across the Internet.

We are all used to using our payment cards, developed for the mundane retail environment, on websites and on the phone. But it makes for an interesting case study to see how, in recent times, PayPal has begun to extend its efforts into physical commerce.

PayPal Here is a payment service provided by PayPal that links buyers and sellers at physical points of inter-action. I tried it out in person at a frozen yoghurt shop in West London (my research budget for this book was a trifle limited).

I ordered a cup of coffee and enquired about the range of payment options. The very friendly and helpful assistant told me that if I used my chip-and-PIN card there would be a 20p surcharge but that if I paid with a card using their PayPal Here reader (a little dongle connected to her iPhone using Bluetooth) there would no charge, a reflection of PayPal's pricing policy. I naturally opted for the latter and the assistant produced an iPhone and ran the PayPal Here app. I put the card into the PayPal Here reader, punched my PIN into the dongle and the transaction was done.

I also tried paying using PayPal instead of a chip-and-PIN card in the same shop. I ran the PayPal app on my iPhone, quickly found the shop I was in and 'checked in' to the location. At this point my picture showed up on the assistant's iPhone and the transaction was completed with the receipt automatically emailed to me.

I asked the shop assistant whether (in essence) she preferred using cards or faces and she said (I'm paraphrasing) that, when it worked, PayPal Here was better. I thought so too. It worked so well that it made me wonder what the point of having the physical card and the card reader was! When the mobile replaces the card and the mobile replaces the terminal, there's no need for the legacy interface.

Using PayPal in physical commerce.

partners and by capturing more information about those partners over time. Thus the cost of trade reduced and the amount of trade went up. Money was an element of these trust networks, because it was cheaper to trust the money than the credit of a counterparty beyond your clan, village or tribe.

Sam had a useful way of thinking about this, which was the idea of what he called 'social hacks' to deal with the historical problem that the speed of bits and the speed of atoms are different. These hacks are things like badges, diplomas, dress codes and, as it happens, banking. Banking grew as a risk intermediary in those trust networks.

However, because of what Sam memorably called the 'superpower' we have gained because we can instantly communicate with anyone else on Earth, we will no longer need those hacks. I may be summarizing incorrectly, but I think his way of looking at the existing business models around identity as being hacks in response to incomplete identity, credential and reputation information is a good way of framing some problems that can be solved using the infrastructure I am suggesting.

A consequence of the ending of the need for such hacks is that social capital will get ever more fungible, so (for example) going to Harvard will mean less than it does now, which means that it will be worth less than it is now. You can see exactly where this headed. Just look at the way we use LinkedIn. In the old world, I would use the social hack of finding out which university your degree came from as a sort of proxy for things I might want to know about you, but I no longer need to do that because from LinkedIn I can find out if you are smart, a hard worker, a team player or whatever. So there's less premium for you learning, say, biochemistry at UCL rather than Swindon Polytechnic: so long as you know the biochemistry, my hiring decision will be tied to your social graph, not the proxy of an institution.

The implications go further. Google was famous for its rigorous hiring criteria, but when they looked at 'tens of thousands' of interview reports and attempted to correlate them with employee performance, they found 'zero' relationship.[44] Their infamous interview brainteasers turned out not to predict anything. Nor did school grade and test scores. The proportion of Google employees with college degrees has decreased over time, a point echoed by Rory Sutherland, the vice chairman of Ogilvy & Mather UK, when he wrote that he was unable to find any evidence that 'recruits with first-class degrees turn into better employees than those with thirds (if anything the correlation operates in reverse)'.[45] Rory suggests the 'Moneyball' approach is better, alluding to Michael Lewis's wonderful book about the transformation of the Oakland Athletics baseball team when they switched to using statistics instead of scouts.[46]

This would now, I suppose, be called a big data approach, and it has tremendous potential to uncover talent. But as Oakland Athletics discovered, that only works so long as you are the only one with the data. In a year or two, everyone else is crunching the same data and applying the same analysis. Maybe analysis will give you your candidate list but the social graph will rank them. In essence, the 'league table' that ranks the candidates will be ranking them by social capital.

But back to ending the 'hacks'. The consequence of most relevance to this book is, of course, that the cost of using social capital will reduce for transactional purposes. In the end it will become lower than the cost of alternatives, the principal alternative at low transaction values being cash. So there will be no need for cash any more. In other words, identity is the new money.

I don't mean this in a metaphorical sense and I don't mean it in the 'big data is the new oil' sense.

I mean it in the very literal sense that the evolution of the identity infrastructure in our online society will mean that there is no longer any need for a circulating medium of exchange in the form of cash.

Sam's framing of 'social hacks' is equivalent to Narayana Kocherlakota's formulation that 'money is technologically equivalent to a primitive version of memory',[47] and Jaron

Lanier's previously mentioned and more recent formulation of economic avatars (i.e. pseudonyms of value in transactional environments) as 'an improvement on the forgetfulness of cash'.[48] Keith Hart saw this coming when at the end of the last century he wrote that, 'If modern society has always been supposed to be individualistic, only now perhaps is the individual emerging as a social force to be reckoned with.' Advances in technology mean that data about the individuals involved in transactions can now be managed at a distance, 'thereby making possible the re-personalisation of complex economic life'.[49]

The key point is that the social graph is a more efficient form of the kind of memory we need to make transactions work. Therefore the social graph will replace the less efficient kinds, of which notes and coins are the principal contemporary example.

It's all about the social costs

Why would we want to replace cash (and cheques)? Jack Dorsey, of Twitter and Square fame, summed the situation up rather nicely in a tweet back in 2012, when he said that, 'in general, the shift toward a cashless society appears to improve economic welfare'. So why are we still using it? That's actually a rather interesting question.

The figures from the UK show that while the use of cash fell 10% at retailers last year, the amount of cash in circulation rose another 6%. This is a consistent pattern. On the one hand we hear that 'cash is king' because the amount of cash in circulation keeps increasing, but on the other hand its use to support commerce keeps falling. So what is all that cash being used for? If you look at the figures you will see (as with comparable

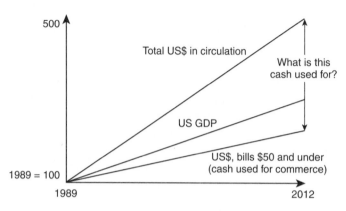

Figure 4.1. The 'cash gap' in the United States.
Source: Federal Reserve Bank of San Francisco Annual Report 2012.

European countries) that the bulk of the growth in cash in circulation is in large-denomination notes. These are not used in retail transactions (indeed, a great many retailers will not accept them) but they are used in a variety of underground transactions: money laundering, corruption, tax evasion and so forth. It is the same situation in the US, as shown in Figure 4.1.

The least efficient transaction mechanism is cash. The cost of producing it, storing it, distributing it, managing it and counting it is vast. It gets lost and stolen. It reduces the costs of crime and enables corruption and tax evasion. Not only are its costs high, but they are unevenly distributed so that the least well-off groups in society pay the highest costs.

Let's get rid of it. Identity means that we don't need it any more, even for those small purchases.

Suppose I am wandering through Woking market and I want to buy a doughnut. I give the trader £1. The trader doesn't have to trust me, he only needs to trust the £1, and the cost of failing to detect that my £1 is a counterfeit is quite small (despite the large number of fake £1 coins in circulation in the UK) compared with the cost of establishing my trust-worthiness and creditworthiness. Other traders deal with this problem by paying banks and card schemes to manage the problem for them, but this costs them money. But now I imagine that I wander up to the trader to buy a hot dog and through his Google Glasses my face is outlined in green, which means that the system recognizes me and that I have good credit. The trader winks at me, and a message pops up on my phone informing me that I am being charged £1. I press 'OK'.

If the trader knew who I was, and remembered me, and trusted me, we could have done all of that without using any of the technology (see the case study on page 67). But now we have the technology, and he doesn't need to remember me or trust me.

Retailers and cash

Retailers are, naturally, central to the replacement of cash for transactions. Generally speaking, retailers mostly talk about payments to complain about the cost of transactions and about card schemes, banks, acquirers and everyone else in the electronic payment value chain. They always say that cash costs next to nothing and that electronic payments should cost even less. Yes, yes. But I think I have detected in occasional conversations that honest retailers are not happy about competing with the dishonest ones who use cash to evade taxes. (This is another excellent reason for making cash reduction an element of national policy.) Getting rid of cash would mean a level playing field.

In 2012 a UK Treasury minister, David Gauke, said that pay-ing tradespersons in cash was morally wrong and that 'home owners who allow workmen to evade VAT or income tax were forcing others to pay more.' His comments attracted a lot of negative comment, even though they are self-evidently true.[51] If a quarter or so of the economy is operating off the books, the rest of us are having to stump up to cover the shortfall.

At a seminar on cashlessness held in Roskilde in Denmark in 2012, a representative of the Danish Chamber of Commerce said they thought that Danish retailers would even be pre-pared to contribute to the cost of the development of the next-generation, new technology retail payment systems. Their view was that retailers are keen on electronic payments as an integrated part of an electronic shopping environment (they meant integrated beyond simple loyalty and coupling; I think they meant discovery, receipts, warranties and so on beyond the POS transaction) and see them as a route to in-creased revenues alongside the cost savings afforded by get-ting rid of cash.

This was an interesting reflection on a mature and reason-able relationship between retailers, banks and society as a whole. If some form of identity infrastructure can provide the 'memory' that retailers need, then we can work with them to eliminate cash and we are all better off.

Linked out

The economist Paul Seabright said that money symbolizes the way we are connected to strangers as never before,[52] so per-haps we should explore how the way these connections are embedded in social graphs is evolving.

I rather like LinkedIn, and use it reasonably often. It's proved a convenient way to build up my network of profes-sional contacts in a very dynamic and usable form. Well, I say 'my' professional contacts, although a UK court has already

Case Study: Ireland without Money

In the decade from 1966 to 1976 there were three major 'all out' bank strikes in Ireland that shut the retail banks for (in total) a year. The way the Irish economy functioned under such duress is both interesting and illustrative.[50] When the strikes hit, around four fifths of the money supply disappeared and the general public were left with the notes and coins in their pockets and nothing else.

Since people could not go to the bank and draw out more money, they developed their own currency substitutes: some people began to use sterling instead, but it was the cheque that kept the economy going. People began to accept cheques directly from each other, and these cheques began to circulate.

In summary, a highly personalized credit system without any definite time horizon for the eventual clearance of debits and credits substituted for the existing institutionalized banking system.

Antoin Murphy points out that one of the key reasons why this 'personalized credit system' could substitute for cash was the local nature of the circulation. This centred on community centres of commerce (i.e. shops and pubs), and because of that the credit risk was minimized. The owners of shops and pubs knew their customers very well and so were perfectly capable of deciding whether to accept cheques (or just IOUs) from those customers. And since the customers also knew each other very well they too could make sensible decisions about which paper to accept.

In 'local' transactions, business can work perfectly well with no currency and no banks. A generation ago Ireland's economy was built up from such local transactions, so people were able to self-organize their own money supply. But, as I think we all understand, in the modern economy 'local' means something entirely different. While none of us know how this is going to pan out, there is clearly a redefinition of locality underway, and it has social networking, virtual worlds and disconnection technologies as inputs. One of my son's localities is World of Warcraft: if Zopa were to offer loans in WoW gold, my son could perform that same function as an Irish publican in the example above and provide an assessment of creditworthiness for avatars he knows.

Until the invention of the mobile phone and its connection with the Internet, it was reasonable to assume that for small transactions there was no way of using identity, credentials and reputation cost-effectively or, indeed, at all. This is why it has made sense to continue to use notes and coins at all to settle retail transactions. But now? The scope to replace notes and coins in this way all hinges on the trader recognizing me. Once this has been achieved, the issue of trust can be instantly resolved by computations across the social graph.

ruled that LinkedIn contacts obtained through my work are, in fact, the property of my employer.

I have a slightly old-fashioned policy towards LinkedIn. When I get a connection request, I won't accept unless it is someone that I've spoken to (or, preferably, met in person). The validity of this policy was demonstrated by the story of the security consultant who set up a fake LinkedIn site for an imaginary woman called 'Robin Sage', who supposedly worked in cybersecurity for the US Navy. In less than a month, she amassed nearly 300 social network connections among security specialists, military personnel and staff at intelligence agencies and defence contractors.[53] The story also revealed a sad truth as well as the potential security risks attendant on social network use: men will do anything for an attractive woman (the profile had such a photo), without even bothering to check whether she's real or not. The non-existent cybersecurity consultant was invited to speak at a conference, review a technical paper, apply for a job and (more than once) dinner.

Given all this, why do I use LinkedIn so much? It's because of the implicit authentication in the social graph. If I am looking for someone to work on a project, or I'm checking up on a job applicant, I use LinkedIn to find out who knows them: and then I contact them. I don't pay any attention to the endorsements. I don't pay any attention to whether I think the person might be real or not, and I don't pay any detailed attention to their academic qualifications. All I pay attention to is the 'trust chain'.

Could this be automated? As Lazlo Bock, the Senior VP of People Operations at Google, has noted, when it comes to hiring decisions, the role of Moneyball-style big data might be limited because organizations are so different.[44] If traversing the trust chain could be automated, it might be far more valuable.

Mobile identity

There's no doubt in my mind that, to be technical for a moment, end-to-end hardware-based encryption and authentication is the most secure, most flexible and most effective security for transactions. Other than issuing custom hardware, there are two other obvious secure computing platforms that are already in customers' hands that could form part of a widespread and standardized identity infrastructure: bank-issued

Case Study: Bank Cards and Identity in Brazil

To see why this is an interesting case study, you need to understand a little about the 'Europay–MasterCard–Visa' (EMV) standard used by the chip-and-PIN cards in your wallet. There are actually three flavours of EMV used by the international card schemes for chip transactions: Static Data Authentication (SDA), Dynamic Data Authentication (DDA), and Combined Data and Application Cryptogram (CDA).

SDA cards are the cheapest, which is why banks started issuing them, but they can be cloned and used in terminals that are offline, so they are a security risk. DDA cards are not vulnerable in this way, but they are more expensive (the cards are more sophisticated – they have a cryptographic co-processor chip built in to handle asymmetric cryptography). The banks in the UK switched to using DDA a couple of years ago. CDA cards are more secure than DDA cards and protect against additional kinds of attack.

Why does it matter to the identity world? Well, if a bank goes to the expense of issuing DDA or CDA cards, then the presence of reusable cryptographic software and the cryptographic co-processor mean that it is a minimum of cost and complexity for the card to carry an additional PKI application (see 'Credentials' in Chapter 3) as well as the EMV application. Almost all of the PKI application's 'guts' are already on the card. In short, a chip-and-PIN card would be a good place to put a cheap identity application for more general use.

Brazil had an ambitious national PKI programme running for a while and is committed to online services and e-government. Banrisul is the largest bank in the south of Brazil, with over 3 million customers, 3,000 ATMs and 100,000 POS terminals. A few years ago, they decided to migrate their payment cards to EMV and they decided to issue CDA cards with enciphered offline PIN (a very secure combination!). So then they began to look around for other applications that they could put on the same card to make it better, deliver new services, reduce churn or whatever might help with the business case.

Meanwhile, back in 2001, the government of Brazil started developing a national PKI (ICP in Portuguese) and had created a national CA together with the legal infrastructure needed to make it all work. About 2 million national certificates have already been issued (in total, not just to Banrisul customers) and these are mainly used for filing tax returns (about 20 million so far).

Banrisul decided to make a PKI application that worked with the national PKI. They put a PKI application with a bank certificate on each card they send out. The customers can then go to a bank branch and use this certificate to obtain a state government certificate (the bank's branches are all RAs) and then use this to obtain a national certificate.

The bank also decided to give out free smart card readers. They are simple, cheap USB readers to work with a browser plug-in. When customers make online transactions using their smart cards, they get higher transaction limits. Customers are therefore using the same card, the same reader and the same PIN to log on to their bank and to buy stuff: a straightforward way to have more security.

EMV cards (see the case study on page 70) and mobile operator-issued SIM cards (see the case study on page 74). This is hardly surprising because EMV cards and SIM cards are actually the same chips but with different application software.

The mobile phone is at the heart of the revolution here. There are a great many reasons why identity based on mobile phones is more secure than identity based on cards, and it's about to get even more secure. The security in a card is based on the physical features of the card and, today, the chip in it. The security in a phone is multidimensional, and therefore so much better. The mobile phone has chips, but it also has a keyboard, screen, apps, memory, interfaces and connectivity.

Now, it is all very well for technologists like me to design a very secure identity scheme based on the security of the mobile handset, but it is another step entirely to work out how to get it into the mass market. Is it something that the mobile operators deliver either individually or in operator consortia? Is it something they do as a joint venture? Or is it for new players to bypass the operators?

National entitlements

Why should we consider bringing together mobile phones and identity? Where will the 'parasitic vitality' come from? What will be the trigger for actually doing something about identity? It may be at hand. As we have seen, the UK government is very muddled about national identity infrastructure. The current system confuses passports and identity cards and entitlements, and consequently delivers few compelling use cases. A future administration will certainly revisit the current arrangements, due to continuing concerns about illegal immigration, health tourism, benefit fraud and so forth.

A good example of these concerns is voting. The British Electoral Commission has just recommended that voters be required to show some form of photographic identification at the ballot box. In most countries this would be uncontroversial, but in the UK we have no photographic identification, so we have to look at co-opting the driving licence infrastructure (as in the US) or the passport infrastructure or consider the introduction of a specific voter's identity card of some kind. None of these are good choices.

Suppose that the vision for national identity (based on the concepts of social graph, mobile authentication, pseudonyms and so on) focused on the certificate rather than on the card or biographical details? Then, as a user of the scheme, I might have a certificate on my purpose-built national entitlement card (so that's some of the population taken care of), I might have entitlement certificates on my bank card (so that's the overwhelming majority of the population taken care of) and I might have certificates in my mobile phone (so that's 99.9% of the population taken care of).

Remember, these certificates would attest to my ability to do something: they would prove that I am entitled to do something (access the NHS, open my office door, buy things in Waitrose), not who I am. They are about entitlement.

The government could give out free smart card readers (as they do in Spain) or leave it to the banks to distribute them. In practice, I think the example set by a modern country such as Turkey (see the case study on page 74) is most attractive: I log in to the government with some ID number, the government sends a message to my mobile phone (over-the-air or via NFC or BLE in the future), the PKI in my SIM decodes the challenge and signs the response, and I'm connected. Securely and simply. And if other service providers want me to log on in the same way, they can issue their own certificates as well.

When it comes to voting, as discussed above, this approach solves many practical problems and, best of all, a phone would be able to check the entitlement presented by another phone, so no one would need special equipment. I show up with my phone and claim that I am entitled to vote: my phone presents a meaningless but unique number, this is entered manually or automatically into the polling clerk's

Case Study: Mobile Phones and Identity in Turkey

Back in 2007, Turkey's largest mobile operator, Turkcell, decided to launch a SIM-based PKI service. It allows subscribers to access securely online services that need strong authentication by using their mobile phone to sign transactions with a legally binding digital signature.

It works in a very simple way (to the customer). When a customer accesses a service that needs authentication, such as logging in to their online bank account or executing a stock trade over the phone, the service requests authentication and a special message is sent via SMS to the customer's handset. Software in the handset intercepts the message and sends it to the PKI application on the SIM card. The message is decoded inside that application and a challenge is extracted. That challenge is then digitally signed using the private key from the application and sent back. When it is received by the service that requested the authentication it can be easily verified as having come from the correct handset, from which the service can infer that the correct PIN had been entered. This is because the public key that corresponds to the private key inside the application is, of course, public.

The consumer sees nothing of this high-grade cryptography in the background. All they see is a message that pops up on their phone and asks them to enter their PIN. After entering the correct PIN, they find they are now logged into their bank or that their transaction has been carried out. Since the SIM card is secure, and the private key used in digital signatures is generated on the SIM and never given up, this is a very safe and secure mechanism.

Within eighteen months of launch Turkcell's service had more than thirty others on board, including a dozen banks and some government bodies.

phone, which flashes up my picture if I am entitled to vote or a red cross if I am not. I show up with my entitlement card and the polling clerk reads it using their NFC interface, and so on. Instead of postal votes, the polling clerk can go to the old folk's home and let them vote individually, certain that they are not being threatened or cajoled.

There's a similar approach to this in Norway (see the case study on page 77) except there the IDs are issued by the banks and used by the government and other private sector organizations. Imagine a national entitlement scheme that used this technology: it would be efficient and cost-effective, since it would use the phones that people already have to deliver services that they definitely want.

Bitcoin, anonymity and privacy

One of the most interesting attempts to deliver a form of cash for the new economy is Bitcoin, the 'cryptocurrency' of the Internet and the subject of intense media attention, and one of its supposed attractions – or flaws – is anonymity.

The best analogy for Bitcoin that I have come up with is the stone currency of Yap. This was explained by the economist Milton Friedman in a famous 1991 paper called 'The island of stone money'.[55] The nation of Yap is a group of four islands in the South Pacific. The islands have no gold or silver or any form of precious metal that could serve the function of money that we are used to. Consequently, where we developed the habit of using metal ingots as stores of value, the inhabitants of Yap used stones. A few centuries ago, they discovered a particular kind of limestone on another group of islands about 250 miles away. Since this limestone was not available on Yap, the supply was limited. From time to time, the tribal chiefs would organize expeditions to these distant islands to quarry and bring back new stones carved into discs. The discs were of various sizes, some only a few inches across and weighing a pound or two, while others could be 12 feet across and weigh thousands of pounds. At the end of a successful expedition the chief who organized it would keep the large stones and 40% of the smaller stones, the remainder being divided between the expedition members. A long-lived and successful chief might therefore have many very large stones outside his house.

Now, suppose that the chief engages in some form of trade or has to pay a large dowry or give a gift to a neighbouring chief for some reason. These large stones are too big to move without considerable effort, so the Yap islanders came up with a practical solution to the problem of minimizing transaction costs. Since the stones were too big to move, they didn't bother. The tribes just agreed that the particular stone no longer belonged to Chief A and now belonged to Chief B instead. Everyone was happy. Over time the stones might be traded again and again, each time staying exactly where they were but with all the tribes agreeing on their new owner. Money is memory, remember, so as long as the tribes could remember which stone belonged to which person, the system functioned perfectly well.

The system worked even when the stones were invisible. Here's what I mean. Suppose the expedition quarried some stones but on the return journey, as would happen from time to time, their raft got caught in a storm and to survive they had to chuck one of the stones off the raft. When they got back to the chief they told him about the stone, which was now five miles down at the bottom of the Pacific. Everyone agreed that the stone still belonged to the chief and when he used that stone in a trade all of the tribes agreed that the

Case Study: Mobile ID in Norway

In Norway, the operator Telenor created an ID company, SETSign, to run a SIM-based PKI. It was very secure and very advanced: but it was very complicated too, and customers ignored it. Actually, lots of them registered for it by SMS when they saw the commercials, imagining, I am sure, that they would get back an SMS saying 'welcome to SETSign' or whatever. In fact, they were sent a multi-page paper form to fill in which, naturally, they didn't. Telenor did not have a choice: they had to send the paper form to gather all of the information they needed to then send on to the bank and comply with regulations. In the end, in a country with 100%+ mobile penetration, only about 2,000 consumers bothered filling out the forms and were accepted by the banks.

Once customers were accepted, their activation codes were sent by registered mail so that customers had to go to the post office with their passports to pick it up. Most of those who were accepted never bothered, and it was clear that the few remaining customers would never generate enough revenue to pay for all of it. The moral of this story might well be: 'don't try and design a security scheme with the cooperation of banks and the post office'!

Telenor decided to try and cut the registration time from six weeks to twenty minutes and eventually got it down to two minutes. They decided that bank security was inappropriate for an average transaction size of €16 (most of which were top-ups). Customers were registered through STK, requiring only their social security number and Visa debit details. Transactions grew from 10,000 per month to 140,000 per month in the first year.[54]

In 2006, Norway's BankID partnership was set up by the Norwegian Financial Services Association (FNH) and the

Norwegian Savings Banks Association along with other banks in the country to establish a national electronic PKI for the banking and finance industry and Telenor decided to work with the BankID consortium to develop an e-signature authentication system for use with mobile handsets.

Norway's second-largest operator, Tele2Norway has launched a similar BankID-compatible mobile ID service to its million Tele2 subscribers giving them the ability to perform secure online transactions through any kind of connected device such as low-end mobile handsets, smartphones or tablets, as long as they use a SIM card. All SIMs in Norway have PKI enabled, which was not hard to coordinate because there are few operators.

My good friend Jon Shamah, an expert on these kinds of schemes, pointed out to me that with this connection to BankID, the registration take up of MobileBankID reached 300,000 users by the end of 2013 and is increasing rapidly. A BankID is issued to each bank account holder in Norway and is used over one million times per day at the time of writing. Mobile users are already seven per cent of BankID users.

stone belonged to the payee. Not only does the stone not go anywhere, none of the participants in the trade has ever even seen it. In a way, and this was Friedman's point: it doesn't really matter whether the stone actually existed or not. Everyone agreed that it did, and therefore it was money.

The tribal chiefs were the central bankers of this system because they organized the quarrying of the stone that brought the new money into existence and the distribution of the stones that formed a rudimentary system of taxation. It all worked reasonably well. It is very interesting to me that the stone money survived the arrival of fiat currency and reports from a few years ago seem to indicate that the value of the large stones had remained fairly stable over time. Interestingly, the 12 foot stone disc weighing thousands of pounds had one very significant advantage over a bar of gold, which is that you can steal a bar of gold but even the most skilled burglar isn't going anywhere with a 12 foot limestone 'coin'.

So this is the analogy with Bitcoin. In Bitcoin, instead of expending manual labour to find a kind of stone that is rare, we expend computing power to find sets of numbers that are rare. These sets of numbers have a particular mathematical property that makes them difficult to find but once you have found them it is easy to check that they have that property, just as the Islanders could easily check that your disc was made from the rare limestone from Palau. Bitcoin releases a twenty-five-coin reward to the first node in the network that succeeds in solving the difficult mathematical problem needed to find the rare numbers. The solution is then broadcast throughout the network, where it can easily be checked, and competition for a new block and its twenty-five-coin reward begins.

As in the case of the stones, if I send you my Bitcoin, the coin isn't really going anywhere (all I'm doing is sending you a copy of the numbers that I found) and we are just telling everybody else that the coin now belongs to you rather than to me. On Yap, the record of ownership of the stones was part of that tribal memory, but in Bitcoin it is the distributed transaction ledger known as the 'block chain'. In essence, when I give you a Bitcoin the record of that transaction is copied out to all of the other users so that everyone now knows that the coin belongs to you. Because of the particular mathematical properties of the numbers used in the Bitcoin system, there is a finite supply (21 million) of these numbers and once they are all discovered no more can ever be 'minted'. It would be as if

Palau had been eroded away by the Pacific storms so that no more limestone discs could enter the Yap economy.

There is one conceptual difference between Bitcoins and stone discs much remarked on in media reports. When it came to the stones, everyone knew to whom the stones belonged. They knew that Stone X belonged to Tribesman A and everyone knew who Tribesman A was. But in Bitcoin, the coins are associated with cryptographic keys rather than individuals. You might know which Internet address one of those cryptographic keys is associated with during a transaction, but that doesn't tell you who the person is. So there is a 'kind of, sort of' anonymity associated with Bitcoin that would have been impossible to imagine for the Yap islanders.

This 'kind of, sort of' anonymity seems to be a focus for the media, with all the talk of the 'Silk Road' market for drugs, etc. One interesting category of criminal enterprise that was linked with Bitcoin is assassination markets, once an enterprising chap by the name of Kuwabatake Sanjuro set one up.[56] In case you're wondering what an assassination market is, it is a prediction market where any party can place a bet (using anonymous electronic money and pseudonymous remailers) on the date of death of a given individual, and collect a payoff if they 'guess' the date accurately. This would incentivize the assassination of specific individuals because the assassin, knowing when the action would take place, could profit by making an accurate bet on the time of the subject's death.

Here's how the market works. Someone runs a public book on the anticipated death dates of public figures. If I hate a particular pop star or politician, I place a bet on when they will die. When the person dies, whoever had the closest guess wins all of the money, less a cut for the house. Let's say I bet £5 that a particular TV personality is going to die on April

Fool's Day 2015. Other people really hate this personality and they put down bets as well. The more hated the person is, the more bets there will be.

April Fool's Day comes around. There's a million pound bet on this particularly personality. I pay a hit man £500K to murder the personality. Hurrah! I've won the bet, so I get the million quid and give half to the hit man. I don't have to prove that I was responsible for the assassination to get the money: I'm just the lucky winner. If someone else had bet 31 March and murdered the television personality themselves the day before, then it would only have cost me a fiver, and I would have regarded that as a fiver well spent.

This is actually rather an old idea. In this form it dates back to 1995 when Jim Bell wrote an essay on 'assassination politics' that brought the idea to the fore, although he wasn't the first person to formulate the post-Internet version of the idea. That was Tim May in his 1994 'Cyphernomicon'. I remember finding the idea intriguing when I first read about it, more for what it said about us (that is, people) than the technology. A society that operated in this fashion would be utterly undesirable. I don't really want to end up in an e-Somalia, at the mercy of competing warlords.

I would have thought Bitcoin is a poor choice for this sort of thing, though, because whatever the media headlines scream, Bitcoin is not terribly anonymous. As *Wired* magazine pointed out some time back, of all the millions of dollars of ransacked Bitcoin out there, none has been spent. The blockchain is public and you can track it until the end of time.

The proponents of retaining cash argue that if e-money advocates like me are to mount a serious effort to eradicate physical money then we must replicate anonymity as it is a key property of cash. I couldn't disagree more. Who would want to live in a society where transactions are anonymous?

Transactions should be private, not anonymous, and this is why the infrastructure for pseudonymity is a more important feature of transactional systems.

When cash is dead

Why the interest in Bitcoin if it isn't the future of cash? I think it points to a latent demand for change. The interest isn't specifically in Bitcoin, to my mind, but rather in the feasibility of an alternative to the state-issued, interest-bearing 'fiat' currency money system that has been in place for the last forty years. The post-industrial economy needs a new kind of money, not one devised by representatives of the status quo: they are the problem, not the solution. In mid 2013, a group of disparate virtual currency groups, ranging from Ven to Bitcoin via Ripple, in fact, came together to form the Digital Asset Transfer Authority (DATA), to support the development of emerging payments using new technologies.

When money settles back down after the discombobulations of the current post-industrial revolution, it will be utterly different.

To begin with, cash will be dead. The disruptive technology has finally arrived, but of course there have to be the right business drivers and the right social drivers to come together for it to actually happen. The business drivers centre on the high cost of cash and the social drivers on the effects of that high cost, which falls mainly on the less well-off who bear the higher transaction costs associated with non-electronic instruments (ATM fees, bus fares to go into town to load cash onto prepaid tokens, cheque cashing fees and so on) and who are excluded from online deals, reduced utility bills for electronic payments, etc.

What is harder to imagine is the impact of the physical medium of exchange vanishing.

Let's take it for granted that the mobile phone takes over and in a few years' time, you will be able to pay Walmart, or your window cleaner, or your niece, with your mobile phone.

In this world, switching between dollars and euros and frequent flier miles and Nectar points and anything else is just a matter of choosing from a menu on the phone. The cost of introducing new currencies will collapse. Anyone will be able to do it. The future of money won't be the single galactic currency of science fiction imagination (we can't even make a single currency work between Germany and Greece, let alone Ganymede and Gamma Centuri) but thousands, even millions, of currencies.

That must sound as crazy to you as the idea of central bank and cheques did to the inhabitants of Stuart England, but it really isn't. Trying to imagine a wallet with a hundred currencies in it and a Coke machine with a hundred slots for them is naturally nuts. But your phone and the Coke machine can negotiate and agree on currencies (or, more importantly, currency markets) in a fraction of a second, the time it takes to 'tap and go' with your Google Wallet.

But who will want to issue these new currencies? Governments? Banks? One obvious category is corporations. When Edward de Bono wrote 'The IBM dollar' back in 1993,[57] he looked forward to a time when 'the successors to Bill Gates will have put the successors to Alan Greenspan out of business', arguing that it would be more efficient for companies to issue money than equity. Another obvious category is communities, especially with sentiments around anti-globalization abounding. Here in London we already have the Brixton e-Pound. The Local Exchange Trading Systems (LETS) from physical communities and the platinum pieces and Facebook credits from virtual communities will merge and surge, forming a panoply of private currencies that will make trade more efficient. Why save dollars for your retirement when you can save kilowatt-hours or calories?

The issues go far beyond economic efficiency and reduced transaction costs. Our view of money will change and, just as the people of Stuart England went from seeing money as coin to money as paper, we will go from seeing fiat currency to seeing a spectrum of currency types that seem alien right now.

Chapter 5

Future and consequences

Electronic transactions have been around for a very long time. The Federal Reserve launched its first dedicated funds transfer network (using Morse Code over fixed lines) almost a hundred years ago, in 1916.[58] Now, though, we have the Internet, mobile phones and biometrics. We have an emerging identity infrastructure that renders the traditional medium of exchange obsolete.

We've also learned lessons from the last time that the banking sector tried to replace the means of exchange using new technology. In hindsight, efforts such as Mondex and Proton, Danmont and VisaCash, might be described as optimally wrong. A bit like chip and PIN, they were designed to succeed in an environment that was on the verge of vanishing, luxury ski runs down a melting glacier. They were designed to flourish in an offline world, just as the world went online.

For reasons already explained, I hesitate to make specific predictions about the more distant future because it is beyond imagination. But I will end here with a few tentative thoughts about future trends.

Let's look out of the corners of our eyes. When it comes to money, I think this means looking away from the world of bank accounts and credit cards, and looking for what Clayton

Christensen would call the disruptive innovation at the bottom of the market.

The divergence of banking and payments

You might have expected more about banks in a book about the future of money. However, banks will not play as big a role in the future of money. The part banks play in our lives could well shrink to taking deposits and creating credit. We all understand that the line between banks and non-banks is blurring in other areas. If the regulation of payments and the regulation of banking diverge, with a lighter touch for payments in contrast to the well-understood demands for tighter regulation in the banking sector, it seems very likely that the business of banking and the business of payments will separate too. We will get a vigorous and innovative payment sector.

Banks will be more tightly regulated because they create money by lending. The world of lending is itself changing, and banks might get squeezed there too. Credit unions could play a huge role in providing an alternative source for lending, but unfortunately they do not have the most efficient infrastructure.[59] With the effective use of mobile as an alternative to cash, their costs should reduce substantially and expand their reach in the UK.

Further, the growth in person-to-person (P2P) lending seems to be successfully coordinating lenders and borrowers via the Internet rather than through institutions. The great success of Zopa, the UK's market leader, is transforming the perception of this sector. It currently provides an average annual return of 4.5% for investors who lend their money to individuals through the platform.[60]

Finally, the provision of capital for business is also ripe for similar coordination. Funding Circle has brokered £47m of small business funding in the past two years. Funding Circle, which facilitates loans to small businesses, advertises an average net return of 5.8%, rising to 14% if investors accept more risk. In a signal turn of events, some local authorities in the UK have now begun to lend to local business through the Funding Circle platform as well.

When it comes to payments, as described earlier there are new technologies that are available to banks and non-banks alike and therefore it is reasonable to speculate as to who might exploit them. What kinds of organizations might step in to provide payment services? In the UK, at least, there's an interesting spread of organizations looking to explore this new frontier. Retail chains, Internet companies, mobile operators and entrepreneurs have all started to play. Since 2011, the UK has seen 38 companies from outside the banking sector take advantage of new EU rules that make it easier to process electronic payments without also offering credit or taking deposits.[61]

Disruption via convenience is inevitable

The technology that is changing money forever is not the smart card and not even the Internet, but the mobile phone. It is personal connectivity that is the currency catalyst, the transforming element. Mobile payment systems have changed the landscape forever in Kenya and the Philippines, but they haven't yet got traction in Western Europe. There was an X-factor missing. Consumers consistently said that they would like to use their phone for payments, but they constantly rejected what they have been offered so far. It just wasn't convenient to send and receive text messages with codes in at the shop counter, even when it did work.

Now, though, we have Near-Field Communication (NFC) and Bluetooth Low Energy (BLE) proximity and vicinity interfaces to integrate the mobile phone into its local environment, forming a bridge between the local and the remote. We have emerging identification infrastructures. We have the 'triple-A' play of authentication, apps and Application Programming Interfaces (APIs). We have our new notion of social identity as the coordinating concept to enable secure and private transactions. The technology components for a truly convenient transactional environment have been coming together for some years, but there needs to be a business rationale too. Here there is the potential for disruptive innovation.

We have the technology enablers, the business push and the social pull of people wanting to use their mobile phones to transact; but the main reason for the resurgence of interest in mobile transactions systems is, in my opinion, a greater readiness to consider radical alternative solutions in the post-crisis landscape. The global credit crunch has left many people feeling that simply patching up the banking system and restoring bonus payments to their pre-crunch levels isn't really a strategic way forward and (because of the increased moral hazard) makes another crisis even more likely. Money and payments are two more aspects of the global financial system that are being re-examined in the light of the global financial crisis.

Banks may not be part of the solution. What if payments just aren't a banking business and the current surge of interest in money and technology reflects this business and social dynamic (since the technology has been in place for a while)?

The reason why there is a resurgence of interest in the future of money is, in an analogous manner, because it is no longer seen as being a state monopoly. Just as we will be using non-bank payment systems to send value around the network, that value will not be the fiat currencies of today.

So we have to imagine, then, a society mediated by connectivity, where interactions take place between social identities, and where commercial transactions can be effected between those social identities using a variety of utilities. What might the implications of this world be? I won't say more here about the technological implications as they have been covered in some detail already. But I will end with some thoughts about what it means for business and for society that identity is the new money.

Business models for new forms of payment

I've already hinted at the potential for a wave of creative destruction – different entities providing different functions all previously put under the heading of banks and money – as the inexorable unbundling of financial services continues. This is not a bad thing.

One lesson from events to date is that a bank could never have triggered the innovation revolution that M-PESA in Kenya clearly did. A key element in its success is that it was born outside the banks and conceived as an infrastructure for others to build on. Mark Pickens makes a point about 'adjacent industries' stimulated by M-PESA and this seems to have led to a high-tech boom in 'Swahili Silicon Valley' around iHub in Nairobi. Cashless schools, pay-for-use water, e-health and an incredible range of applications have been made possible by the ready availability of a mass-market payment system for the twenty-first century. As the CEO of Kenya Commercial Bank is quoted as saying, when asked if M-PESA is a threat to banks, 'If you don't respond it's a threat, but if you embrace it, then it's an opportunity.' I see this as a template for payment system evolution in Europe and maybe in the US as well.

Finally, I cannot help but note how this example reinforces the relationship between identity and money. One of the most unexpected impacts of M-PESA was the use of M-PESA transaction histories as substitutes for conventional credit ratings. Remember that many M-PESA agents are merchants, so it is natural for them to extend credit in this way. In other words, M-PESA became a means for previously excluded people to demonstrate identity and reputation. Paul Makin, the head of Consult Hyperion's Mobile Money practice (and the chap who carried out the original feasibility study on behalf of Vodafone), and I have discussed this many times.

M-PESA has another valuable lesson. I can see a future in which the regulator insists on interoperability between mobile money schemes and regulates the interchange rates, but some players want more than this, and in this they adumbrate skirmishes about to break out in developed markets. Tensions arise from Safaricom's control of the SIM card, because the banks want (but haven't got) access to it. I can remember from the early days of the project that there was considerable debate about how to implement the service for consumers. Consult Hyperion recommended going down the hardware security route (i.e. using the SIM card). This meant writing new 'SIM Toolkit' software and re-issuing Safaricom SIMs to customers who wanted to use mobile payments. Safaricom decided to make the investment required to go down this high-security route rather than use SMS or USSD, hoping that it would act as an anti-churn factor in a SIM-based market. This was at the time a brave decision, but one that has been repaid many times over. Good for them. I can't see how regulators can realistically force operators to open up the SIM for more SIM Toolkit applications. But as in the case of smartphone applications in developed countries it might be realistic to ask the operators to agree on a standard, SIM-based identity management infrastructure and then provide open, transparent and non-discriminatory access to it. But that's another story.

Why cash replacement is a forerunner
of identity-based transactions

Remember that *Los Angeles Times Magazine* prediction about 2013? It included a trip to the ATM to draw out cash.

> After parking the van, Alma stops for some cash at the bank-teller machine in the lobby of her building. She punches in her I.D. number and then puts her thumb on the screen. After several tries, the machine finally recognizes her finger-print and gives her two $20 bills with bar codes that verify the money has been issued to her.

The last time I went to the US, I paid for everything using cards and my mobile phone (Starbucks, LevelUp and Google Wallet). Yet I read only recently, in a discussion about the near future,[64] that

> There's some debate about whether plastic credit and debit cards will be totally replaced by mobile payment systems in the next few years. However, there's no doubt that, in 2030, my son will carry a wallet with cash in it, because we'll still be using paper and metal money well into the future.

That leads me to speculate that there might be a social class element to the money transactions roadmap. Perhaps in another quarter of a century, the middle classes will have abandoned cash and it will exist only to serve the poor and excluded. That is a plausible scenario, but I do not think we will see it. The device formerly known as the mobile phone is a way to accept payments as well as make them, and this is what will do for cash.

The UK media reaction to the suggestion that cheque clearing might be abandoned in a decade is illustrative. 'How will I pay my cleaning lady?' was the typical insurmountable hurdle to change identified in the pages of the *Daily Telegraph*. This strikes me as exactly analogous to those mid-1980s comments about mobile phones, along the lines of: 'Well if I want to make a phone call when I am out, I can always use a payphone.' Just for the record, I pay our cleaner using my bank's mobile app and the money is sent via the Faster Payment Service (FPS).

People thought plastic cards would one day replace cash, but this never happened because while it was very easy to issue cards to everybody it was not possible to give all of them terminals to accept cards. The mobile phone has profoundly altered this dynamic because it can replace both the plastic card and the terminal for accepting plastic cards. It's this latter point that is truly disruptive.

Tally sticks turned the mechanism for deferred payment into a store of value. The cheque turned the store of value into a means of exchange. The gold standard created a stable unit of account. None of these implementations are laws of nature. They depend on technology push and the societal pull.

Today, I think we are in the same position as the medieval court experimenting with tally sticks or industrializing England paralysed by pre-industrial means of exchange. We have a paradigm mismatch that explains the mid-life crisis: money feels out of place, unconnected, uncomprehending. We're using the mentality of coins and the institutions of paper to try and deliver the money for a new economy. In Japan and South Korea, where mobile phones have been used for payments for some time, we can see the shape of the adoption curve. It's linear on the consumer side and flat on the retailer side, until about a third of consumers have the technology. Then we get the 'hockey stick' that we technologists love. While these countries are often the focus of attention for people looking at the future of mobile, I think that Kenya, in allowing a disruptive new entrant, has more lessons for the UK.

Social currencies

I'd like to end with some thoughts about how the nature of money might impact society. To use the postmodern visualization of Umberto Eco, we shouldn't be designing virtual cash, but hypercash: not an electronic version of cash as it currently is, but an electronic version of money (cash and non-cash transactions) as it should be. I'm not advocating the construction of fantasy money that disconnects from the real world (Eco warns of the dangers of feeling 'homesick for Disneyland' in *Travels in Hyperreality*, which was one of those books you enjoy reading, but at the end realize that you haven't understood). We should be able raise the bar higher than an electronic simulation of the plastic simulation of the paper simulation of money that we have now. This means 'cash' that implements privacy, as mentioned in the discussion about Bitcoin, but it also means currencies that embody different values.

Currencies? Yes. One of the questions often asked is whether the dynamic of monetary evolution is a tendency to one currency (the galactic credit beloved of science fiction authors) because the minimization of global transaction costs is the driving factor or an explosion of currencies because new technology minimizes transaction costs in other ways. As noted already, as a technologist, I suspect that there will be more different kinds of money, not just more currencies, than ever before. The cash replacement technologies discussed earlier this book – PayPal and M-PESA, iDEAL and EMV – do not understand that sterling is a 'real' currency and World of Warcraft Gold is not. Surely a key impact of the transition to efficient electronic platforms, rather than bits of paper, is that currency is just another field in the dataset: I could use PayPal to send Dave's dollars as easily as sending US dollars.

The new local

In the Long Finance exploration of the world of financial services in 2050, 'In Safe Hands', written by Gill Rowland, the 'Many Hands' scenario (see Figure 5.1) with city states replacing nation states as the basis of society and commerce seems to me the most likely.[62] This panders to my long-held appreciation of Jane Jacobs's work on the city as the basic economic unit.

A world economy built up from cities and their hinterlands will obviously demand different financial services and institutions from one based on national economies. What this means to me is that the future sense of identity will be city-centric, with people seeing themselves as Londoners and New Yorkers rather than Brits and Yanks. Cities will undoubtedly form defence alliances and trade pacts and so forth with each other but I wonder if they will give up any real sovereignty? It's an interesting and enjoyable area of speculation.

In discussing that C50 scenario, Gill makes a passing but powerful observation on this future, saying that individuals will protect their 'personal identity, credit ratings and parking spaces' at all costs and that since monetary arrangements (nation-state fiat currencies) will have collapsed, the commercial paper of global corporations will be used as international currency.

Thanks to www.longfinance.net

Figure 5.1. Long Finance scenarios for 2050.

I might take issue with Gill here and say 'social identities' but I know what she means. Credit rating – referring to the commercial reputation that means that you can buy or sell, whether an individual or an organization – will be central to economic existence. In a networked society, this is more likely to be something that comes from the social graph than the conventional credit rating of today, as discussed above.

In the language of digital identity, digital money and digital networks, Gill is predicting a reputation economy anchored in the mundane, a world in which the monetary guidebooks are already at hand. These include Hayek's *The Denationalization of Money* and De Bono's CSFI pamphlet *The IBM Dollar* (both of which you can find reprinted in David Boyle's 'The Money Changers') and take us through a landscape animated by new technology but shaped by physical as well as virtual communities.

This will be a wholly different economy. We will have multiple identities, use multiple monies (but not cash), through services provided by different entities, and be defined by our social network and reputation. There will be social and political implications impossible to foresee clearly. But we do know that we will, if anything, be underestimating the long-term implications of these changes.

What is to be done? Predictions are hard, especially about the future, as the old saying goes.

We technologists are well aware that we overestimate how fast new technologies will be adopted but underestimate their long-term impact. In other words, it may take longer than people like me think for identity infrastructure to remove cash from our everyday lives, but when it does the impact on society will be far greater than mass redundancies in the ATM business.

So perhaps the idea that 'alternative' money can work in isolated local environments but not at scale is wrong, because both locality and globalization now mean something different and there's no reason why interconnection between local money of one form or another (via markets) cannot operate globally. I'm not thinking about Lewes Pounds or LETs here, but mobile minutes, bandwidth and Tesco money. Next time the banks collapse, or sterling becomes worthless, we will get a chance to try some of these ideas out.

At the end of the transition to e-money, the marginal cost of introducing another currency will be approximately zero. So we will be in the 'let a thousand flowers bloom' mode and might reasonably expect a rash of experimentation. At the end of this period, who knows whether dollar bills or Bill's dollars (an old joke, beloved of us e-cash types) will be more successful?

What might the far future look like? Hayek pointed out a generation ago that people who lived in 'border areas' in days of old seemed perfectly capable of understanding multiple monies (and surely we are all on the border now: the border between the physical world and cyberspace) so there's no reason to think that they couldn't do so again. More importantly, however, the exchange of medieval moolah took place without mobile phones and 24/7 FX markets.

If I've already told my mobile phone that I want to collect US dollars because I'm going to go on holiday to New York as well as World of Warcraft Gold pieces because I feel like a relaxing weekend of Orc slaughter, then my mental transaction cost subsequently falls to zero. My mobile phone is perfectly capable of negotiating with yours:

Have you got any WoW Gold?

No, will you take British Airways Avios?

Yes, but as they are worthless junk it will be at a 95% discount.

Alright, here you go...

I think the traditional view of the link between geography and currency is too restrictive: perhaps in the future, all money will be local, it's just that local will mean something different in the connected world. Reed's Law readies will all be local to someone, so perhaps community currency might be the best description. Whether the community is Totnes or the Chinese diaspora (an example of what Gill refers to as 'affinity groups') or World of Warcraft won't matter, but the shared desire to minimize transactions costs for 'us' at the possible expense of transactions costs from 'them' will. Since the overwhelming majority of retail transactions are local, most people's transactions most of the time will be in their local currency with minimal transaction costs. A small but growing number (because of online commerce) of transactions will be in 'foreign' currencies (i.e. someone else's local currency).

This is more of a reconnection with the past than it may seem at first. If we look at the history of money management by ordinary people, the relative use of the money instruments available becomes fascinating. In Britain, for example, right up to the nineteenth century, there were normally several currencies in circulation in addition to sterling. This situation, having been temporarily banished by state capitalism in the post–Bretton Woods world, is likely to be restored.[63]

The long-term outcome will surely be that technology is not used to develop replicants – electronic means of exchange that simulate, as perfectly as possible, the current physical means of exchange – but to develop new means of exchange that are better for society as a whole. Thus e-money as a vehicle for Szabo-style synthetic currencies that could be used directly in contracts as payments ought to be the science fiction writers' new monetary paradigm. No more 'that will be ten galactic credits, thank you,' more 'you owe me a return trip to Uranus and a kilogram of platinum for delivery in 12 months.'

OK, so what?

I hope that I have persuaded you that we are about to see really big changes in the way that individuals and organizations transact. We can let these changes go, or we can try and use them to everyone's benefit. I'd like to suggest three ways in which we could exploit the new technology in the UK in specific and beneficial ways.

We need to begin by finding a way to make the construction and use of a new infrastructure for identity a national project of significance. We need to find something that can provide the 'parasitic vitality' for a new identity paradigm. We already know that in the UK, as well as in the US, Australia and many other countries, there is no appetite for any kind of national identity scheme. But there may be an alternative formulation – the National Entitlement Scheme mentioned in Chapter 4 – that helps all stakeholders: individuals, businesses, governments, law enforcement and everyone else. Long before the late and unlamented national identity scheme in the UK, there was (back in 2002) the original proposal for an entitlement card. This should be revisited in the light of modern technology.

The demands for 'something to be done' are growing. The reason I say this is, without making a political point, that it is impossible to balance uncontrolled mass migration, the nature of modern working life and the British welfare state. There is no need to explore this point further here, except to say that a great many people would be in favour of welfare claimants having to present their entitlement to welfare, patients having to present their entitlement to health services, voters having to present their entitlement to exercise the franchise and so on. We can use the modern privacy-enhancing infrastructure to decouple these entitlements from the underlying identities and resolve the paradox of more security and privacy.

When the original discussions about an Entitlement Card took place, the government was imagining a more or less conventional Victorian-style index card. We are long past that point. We should use the identity assurance programme currently being developed by the Cabinet office (the IDA) to implement the entitlement scheme. As a citizen I might decide to carry around my entitlements on a card, or I might more likely leave the card at home in a drawer and carry the entitlements around in my phone.

This approach would stimulate banks, mobile operators, service providers and everyone else who wants a better identity infrastructure to cooperate in animating the right kind of identity infrastructure. When you walk into a pub and are asked to prove that you are over 18 then you will be able to use your mobile phone to do just that: not to prove who you are, or prove that you can drive, or declare your immigration status, but through the magic of cryptography provide proof that you are of legal age to drink. Similarly when I log on to make an appointment with my doctor, or visit a polling booth or pop down to sign on the dole, like 90% of the population I will use my mobile phone to prove entitlement.

One very specific use of the new infrastructure should be to greatly reduce the cost and complexity of executing transactions in the UK by explicitly recognizing that reputation will be the basis of trust and therefore transaction costs. The regulators should therefore set in motion plans for a Financial Services Passport. This would use the same infrastructure as the National Entitlement Scheme but with a sector-specific profile. The UK's IT industry trade association, TechUK, has a working group looking at just this idea already and together with colleagues at Consult Hyperion we have put forward the same suggestion to the Federal Reserve in response to their November 2013 consultation on the evolution of the US Payments System.

At root, the concept is to have some kind of 'money name' that might be more convenient for consumers than either bank account numbers or mobile phone numbers. The equivalent of a Twitter name or Facebook name might make sense, so I might ask people to send money to £dave or log in to get an insurance quote as £dave and so on. This might be better labelled a 'financial services identifier' (FSI), that could be bound with appropriate credentials – post customer due diligence (CDD) – to form a secure financial services passport which could then be used to effect considerable cost reductions in the financial services industry as a whole and shift more transactions online.

The easiest way to do this would be to assign an FSI to a person or other legal entity the first time that they go through a CDD process. Once someone has one of these FSIs, then there would be no need for them to go through CDD again at other institutions. This would greatly reduce industry costs and make it simpler and cheaper and more convenient to engage in any kind of financial transaction, e.g. obtaining a new bank account, credit card, insurance policy, accountant, and so on. It doesn't matter if a person has multiple FSIs, because each FSI will have been obtained as the result of a CDD process. Consumers might want to have a personal financial persona and a small business financial persona that point to a personal and to a business account and use them for different purposes, for example.

Since the financial services passport would be using the same infrastructure as the entitlements scheme, one might expect the costs to be manageable and the cost savings to UK plc significant.

Finally, I should like to make a rather technical and boring plea to the relevant authorities to make the UK's National Payments Plan adopt an explicit target for reducing the total social cost of payments in the UK. This will inevitably mean coming up with tactics to reduce cash (and cheque) usage in the UK.

These are straightforward calls to action and I trust that you have been persuaded to support them!

Glossary

BLE   Bluetooth Low Energy

BRC   British Retail Consortium

C50   The 50 richest 'city states' that might exist in 2050

CA   Certification Authority

CIT   Cash in Transit

DAG   Digital Asset Grid

DVLA   Driver and Vehicle Licensing Agency

DWP   Department for Work and Pensions

ECB   European Central Bank

EMV   The international standard for payment using smart cards (so named because it was originally developed by Europay, MasterCard and Visa)

GPS   Global Positioning System

HMRC   Her Majesty's Revenue & Customs

IDA   The (UK government) Identity Assurance programme

IP   Internet Protocol

IVR   Interactive Voice Response

MBUN   Meaningless but Unique Number

M0   The narrow money supply comprising the total value of notes and coins in issue

NFC   Near-Field Communication

NSTIC The (US government) National Strategy for Trusted Identities in Cyberspace

PET Privacy-Enhancing Technology

PKC Public-Key Certificate

PIN Personal Identification Number

PKI Public-Key Infrastructure

RA Registration Authority

SIBOS SWIFT International Banking Operations Seminar

SIM Subscriber Identification Module, the chip inside a digital mobile phone that links the device to a user

SMS Short Message Service (the GSM text message service)

SWIFT Society for Worldwide Interbank Financial Telecommunication

TTP Trusted Third-Party

WPS Witness Protection Scheme

Endnotes

1. E. Finch. 2003. What a tangled web we weave: identity theft and the Internet. In *Dot.cons: Crime, Deviance and Identity on the Internet* (ed. Y. Jewkes), ch. 6. Cullompton, Devon: Willan.

2. R. Watson. 2011. Scenarios for the future of money. The Digital Money Forum, March.

3. D. S. Schlichter. 2011. Beyond the cycle: paper money's endgame. In *Paper Money Collapse: The Folly of Elastic Money and the Coming Monetary Breakdown*. Hoboken: John Wiley.

4. B. Steil. 2007. The end of national currency in foreign affairs. The Council on Foreign Relations, May.

5. M. Klein. 2000. Banks lose control of money. *Financial Times*, 15 January.

6. T. Levinson. 2009. The undoing of the whole nation. In *Newton and the Counterfeiter*. London: Faber & Faber.

7. D. Birch. 2001. Farewell then, Beenz. *Guardian*, 27 September.

8. D. Birch. 2000. Reputation not regulation. *Guardian*, 2 November.

9. S. Lessin. 2013. Identity+30. In South-by-Southwest Interactive, March.

10. J. Weatherford. 1998. The fiscal frontier. *Discover*, October.

11. A. Murphy. 1978. Money in an economy without banks. *The Manchester School* 46(1).

12. E. Dyson. 2001. Who am I talking to? *New York Times Syndicate*, 21 May.

13. Break the law and your new 'friend' may be the FBI. Associated Press (16 March 2010).

14. J. Clippinger. 2007. The power of identity narratives. In *A Crowd of One: The Future of Individual Identity*. New York, NY: Public Affairs.

15. M. Lloyd. 2003. Murder at the opera. In *The Passport*. Stroud: Sutton.

16. P. Clements. 1999. The British and the Risorgimento. *History Review*, 1 December.

17. J. Agar. 2001. Modern horrors: British identity and identity cards. In *Documenting Individual Identity*. Woodstock, UK: Princeton University Press.

18. N. Sibley. 2008. The passport system. *Journal of the Society of Comparative Legislation* 7(1):26.

19. V. Groebner. 2007. Major apparatuses. In *Who Are You? Identification, Deception and Surveillance in Early Modern Europe*. Brooklyn, NY: Zone.

20. N. Gilbert. 2007. *Dilemmas of Privacy and Surveillance – Challenges of Technological Change*. Royal Academy of Engineering, March.

21. C. Edwards and C. Fieschi. 2008. UK Confidential. Demos, May.

22. D. Birch and A. Krotoski. 2007. Eavesdropping on the future of identity. In *Digital Identity Management: Technological, Business and Social Implications*. Aldershot, UK: Gower.

23. D. Solove. 2007. Anonymity and accountability. In *The Future of Reputation*. New Haven, CT: Yale University Press.

24. W. Sofsky. 2008. Property. In *Privacy – A Manifesto*. Princeton, NJ: Princeton University Press.

25. H. Clinton. 2011. Internet rights and wrongs: choices & challenges in a networked world. Delivered at George Washington University on 15 February.

26. C. Robertson. 2010. Introduction. In *The Passport in America*. New York: Oxford University Press.

27. D. Edmonds. 2013. Twelve billion fingerprints. *Prospect*, June.

28. J. Grijpink and C. Prins. 2001. New rules for anonymous electronic transactions? *Dutch Journal of Private Law* 4.

29. D. Birch and N. McEvoy. 2007. A model for digital identity. In *Digital Identity Management: Technological, Business and Social Implications*. Aldershot, UK: Gower.

30. R. Clarke. 2001. The fundamental inadequacies of conventional PKI. ECIS, June.

31. J. Lanier. 2013. Financial identity. In *Who Owns the Future?* London, UK: Allen Lane.

32. E. Schonfeld. 2012. 61% of Disqus comments are made with pseudonyms. AOL, 9 January.

33. J. Crosby. 2008. Challenges and opportunities in identity assurance. HM Treasury, March.

34. J. Bender. 2008. The German eID card. The European e-Identity Conference, June.

35. J. Beddington. 2013. Foresight future identities. The Government Office for Science, January.

36. A. Krotoski. 2013. A nation of narcissists. In *Untangling the Web.* London: Faber & Faber.

37. Mexico: The use of government databases by third parties to locate persons via UNHCR:MEX103805.E. At http://www.refworld.org/docid/50754ab62.html, 31 December 2013.

38. S. Landau. 2013. Politics, love and death in a world of no privacy. *IEEE Security & Privacy*, May.

39. G. Marx. 2001. Identity and anonymity: some conceptual distinictions and issues for research. In *Documenting Individual Identity: The Development of State Practices in the Modern World.* Princeton, NJ: Princeton University Press.

40. B. Schneier. 2000. Certificates and credentials. In *Secrets and Lies: Digital Security in a Networked World.* New York, NY: Wiley Computer Publishing.

41. D. Edgerton. 2006. Significance. In *The Shock of the Old.* London: Profile Books.

42. G. Davies. 1995. The Treasury and the tally. In *A History of Money: From Ancient Times to the Present Day.* Cardiff: University of Wales Press.

43. C. Shenton. 2012. Worn-out, worm-eaten, rotten old bits of wood. In *The Day Parliament Burned Down.* Oxford University Press.

44. A. Bryant. 2013. In head-hunting, big data may not be such a big deal. *New York Times*, 19 June.

45. R. Sutherland. 2013. Why I'm hiring graduates with thirds this year. *The Spectator*, 6 July.

46. M. Lewis. 2003. How to find a ballplayer. In *Moneyball: The Art of Winning an Unfair Game*. New York, NY: W. W. Norton.

47. N. Kocherlakota. 1998. Money is memory. *Journal of Economic Theory* 81:232–51.

48. J. Lanier. 2013. Financial identity. In *Who Owns The Future?* London, UK: Allen Lane.

49. K. Hart. 1999. Money in the age of the Internet. In *The Memory Bank*. London, UK: Profile.

50. A. Murphy. 1978. Money in an economy without banks. *The Manchester School* 46.

51. C. Hope. 2012. It is 'morally wrong' to pay tradesmen cash in hand, says David Gauke. At http://www.telegraph.co.uk/finance/personalfinance/consumertips/tax/9421590/Middle-classes-who-pay-cash-in-hand-morally-wrong-and-aiding-law-breaking-says-minister.html, 23 July.

52. P. Seabright. 2005. Money and human relationships. In *The Company of Strangers: A Natural History of Economic Life*. Woodstock, UK: Princeton University Press.

53. S. Waterman. 2010. Ficticious femme fatale fooled cybersecurity. *The Washington Times*, 18 July.

54. H. Sjursen. 2005. Cooperation for mobile payments in Norway. *Mobile Payments*, March.

55. M. Friedman. 1991. The island of stone money. The Hoover Institution, E-91-3.

56. A. Greenberg. 2013. Meet the 'assassination market' creator who's crowdfunding murder with Bitcoins. At http://www.forbes.com/sites/andygreenberg/2013/11/18/meet-the-assassination-market-creator-whos-crowdfunding-murder-with-bitcoins/, 23 November.

57. E. de Bono. 2002. The IBM dollar. In *The Money Changers*. London: Earthscan.

58. E. Solomon. 1998. Money on the move. In *Virtual Money*. New York: Oxford University Press.

59. W. Clinton and A. Schwarzenegger. 2008. Beyond payday loans. *The Wall Street Journal*, 24 January.

60. E. Moore. 2013. Risk and reward in the P2P revolution. *Financial Times*, 26 July.

61. B. Masters and E. Moore. 2013. 'E-money' challenge for high street banks. *Financial Times*, 14 April.

62. G. Ringland. 2011. In safe hands? The Future of Financial Services. SAMI Consulting Ltd, December.

63. K. Hart. 1999. The future of money and the market. In *The Memory Bank*. London, UK: Profile.

64. From http://gizmodo.com/5933276/15-current-technologies-well-still-be-using-in-2030 (accessed 26 July 2013).